The Jew A Negro

THE JEW A NEGRO

BEING

A STUDY OF THE JEWISH ANCESTRY

FROM AN IMPARTIAL STANDPOINT.

———o———

BY

ARTHUR T. ABERNETHY, A.M., Ph.D.

(Mem. A. L., A. A. A. S.)

AUTHOR OF

"Did Washington Aspire to be King?"
"History of New York" (3 vols.)
"Mechanics of Electric Telegraph,"
"King Leopold in the Congo,"
"History of the Theatre,"
"Bertie and Clara,"
"Autobiography of a Madman," etc.

———

DIXIE PUBLISHING COMPANY,
MORAVIAN FALLS, N. C.
1910

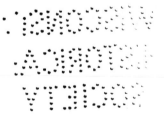

THIS BOOK

IS AFFECTIONATELY DEDICATED TO

MR. WALTER BURNS,

OF PHILADELPHIA, AND TO HIS BEAUTIFUL WIFE,

ADA TERRY BURNS,

IN GRATEFUL APPRECIATION OF THE MANY HOURS OF

GENIAL HOSPITALITY ENJOYED IN THEIR HOME.

PREFACE.

THIS WORK must not be misinterpreted into an attack upon the Hebrew race. That its undeviating title may presuppose such a condition, the Author feels certain; that the Author intends to reflect the slightest personal or historical discredit upon this peculiar people he emphatically denies. It is the duty of history to chronicle events—and incidents connecting with individuals or nationalities which create events—without the slightest suggestion of favor, fear or suspicion. Cicero, the Roman, said: "It is the first and fundamental law of history that it should neither dare to say anything that is false, nor fear to say anything that is true, nor give any just suspicion of favor or disaffection." What is written here is based on the Author's unprejudiced researches among historians who have both favored and criticised the Jews as a race, and their principal historical characters as individuals.

The Jew has had high place in the history of the world. He has figured in the military, political, social, religious enterprises of almost every country. He has been characteristically nomadic; going from place to place, and taking active part in the affairs of state everywhere, but building no kingdom of his own.

From the earliest days of the race, when Menes (said by some to have been from the loins of Ham while accredited as the offspring of Shem by equally eminent historians) first occupied the throne of Egypt, to the days when Joseph formed the first money, stock and land trust by effecting a corner on all the food products of Egypt's fertile country, and requiring of his Jewish brethren their lands, money, and, in many instances, their families as remuneration to Pharaoh—aye, even to the days of the modern Rothschilds—the Jews have been prominent in the conduct of state in nearly every nation.

Abraham was everywhere counselling with the monarchs of nations through which he migrated, and he not infrequently found it to his advantage to juggle the truth which he unhesitatingly did on two occasions to save himself from the unpleasantness of being put to death. We find Ezra, a scribe of Moses, exercising great authority under Cyrus when he was King of Persia. Daniel had already served uninterruptedly as Babylon's Prime Minister for the remarkable space of sixty-five years when Darius with his ally Cyrus destroyed the Kingdom of Babylon and promoted Daniel to even higher place of state by making him chief of three presidents to whom he had distributed the government of his great empire. The history of Egypt began and ended with Hebrew blood in control; and we find the Jews vacillating between high place and the penitentiary in almost every instance. Joseph's impetousity got him into jail in Egypt. The courtiers of Darius

threw Daniel into the den of lions although their predecessors had previously engaged him in a still more
effective test of personal courage by having thrown him
into a fiery furnace whence he had escaped unharmed.

When Ahasuerus, ruler from India even to Ethiopia,
with his one hundred and twenty-seven provinces
was on his throne in Shushan, he grew a little too
merry under the mellowing influences of his wine-feast
and commanded his voluptuous Vashti to appear before
the company of princes he was dining that they, too,
might observe her ravishing charms. We are told that,
because she also having entertained the noble women of
the realm until the pleasantries had flown to her head,
and not being inclined to yield to her merry-making
lord refused peremptorily to come into him, she
was deposed from her reginal title, and a certain
Jew, Mordecai, a Benjamite, for whom a hang-
man's scaffold was within the month to be erected,
worked his way into the graces of Ahasuerus and
dictated the selection of a kindred Jewess, Esther.
That this Jew accomplished his purposes with the
characteristic Hebrew skill and diplomacy is evident from the haste with which the royal mon-
arch forgot his beauteous Vashti, and "speedily
gave her her things," and, as it is further said, "The
king loved Esther above all the women," which was a
very unique compliment and distinction as he had a
splendid assortment always on hand and Vashti was
regarded as incomparable in charms. Mordecai was
not long in being called to the place of his uncompro-

mising rival, Haman, as a chief advisor to the king, and he celebrated his authority by hanging the blundering Haman on the scaffold Haman had so cheerfully constructed for the elusive Jew. And so the history goes.

For those who perceive a difference in the capabilities of the Negro as compared with the Jew the Author recommends a more extensive study of the conditions of the Negro than may be procured from observations of the American Negro alone. Indolence, shiftlessness, and their concurrent ill qualities are results of climatic conditions, not of traits of blood. Besides, the American Negro has but lately emerged from slavery; he has known only the soil while his more fortunate kinsman, the Jew, has from his early nomadic disposition, acquired the languages and arts of the traveler and tradesman and has trafficked in merchandise where his wits have been more sharpened.

What the Author claims in this work is, not that the Jew is inferior; nor does he wish to impute to the Jewish race any of those objectionable traits claimed by the Caucasian to be found in the Negro type of humanity. Subjects of ethnology must be considered above racial prejudices. The ethnologist, like the laws which govern nature, must be no respecter of persons. Whatever may be the claim of pre-determined historians as to the Negro, we must consider him as a race rather than as an individual tribe or community. Besides, it is not a fair parallel to draw to study the Jew and the Negro in comparison alone with the American Negro. The best examples of the Author's contention are found directly in Northeastern Africa where they have dwelt in their native originality and simplicity of custom, habits, etc., since the days when Ethiopians first governed imperial Egypt.

The effort of the Author is to prove herein, by evidence from history showing the intermingling of the Jewish race with those of other races, and these, in turn, with still other races, together forming a miscellaneous intermingling of racial affinities, that the Jew of to-day, as well as his ancestors in other times, is the kinsman and descendant of the Negro, holding the Negro's features and characteristics through the long years of racial transmutations, and (I might add) *in spite of* the Jewish intermarriages into other races which fact is so thoroughly established by history.

*An impartial authority of international repute, one of the greatest in the world as an anthropologist and ethnologist, recently wrote the Author: "As for the Jew, there is one man, Dr. Maurice Fishberg of New York, himself a Jew, who has been making a splendid study of his race, sociologically and ethnically. His articles appear mostly in Popular Science Monthly, edited by Professor J. McKeen Cattell, of Columbia University.

"His conclusions as to racial affinities are startling but true and prove to be so. The Jew in physique is the same as the races among which he lives. He is broad headed among broad headed races(Russia,) and long headed among long headed (Africa and Spain.) *There is no modern Jewish race.* Intermarriage causes this, and the Jew type disappears if there ever was one. In Russia, I am told by a Jew, it was customary to disinherit the first born, because of the *jus primae noctis* custom. Hence this alone brought new blood in. The Rabbi in this city is from Northern Germany, and is a typical blond Aryan. Jews in Algeria are of the Mediterranean race. They have long ceased to be a "people," and have become a religious sect; and they desert their religion whenever they can because they are no longer adjusted to it. Religions are ethnic matters after all is said, so they tend to become allied to the church of the people among whom they live—when they have liberty to do so.

"Originally they were a small piece of the Semitic speaking people, and there is some evidence that the whole Mediterranean basin, or at least much of it, was Semitic before the Aryans came down. There is also some evidence of a relation between the Hamitic and Semitic languages, proving that the two are sisters of the same parents and the parent was the great Mediterranean race, which includes Arabs, Egyptians, Berbers, Ancient Spaniards, Ligurians, Pelasgians, and all the other tribes living around the Mediterranean.

"Now for the early affinity of the Negro: the best book, I guess, is that of Professor G. Sergi, of University of Rome: "The Mediterranean Race." An English translation is published in New York, I think, by Macmillan. He proves what many another anthropologist has done before, namely, that all the long-headed types

in Africa and Europe are closely related. The head
shape is identical or nearly so, from the Negro to the
Scandinavian, and there is a perfect gradation of complexion and other characters, from the little, black
broad-nosed Negro to the big, white, narrow nosed
Scandinavian. The broad heads in Europe are all in-
truders from Asia. I do not agree with him that this
race (Eur-African) arose in Africa and spread North,
but the opposite is the truth. Nor do I agree with him
that the original Aryans were the broad headed Asiatic
invaders. The weight of evidence is to the effect that
the original Aryan was the blond part of this Eur-
African race which was cooped up in the North; the
original Semites were those which spread around the
Mediterranean—probably on the Northern and Eastern
shores. The Hamites were, then, an early offshoot in
Africa. It is but a step from the Berber and Egyptian
to the Sandanese and from these to the true Negro. All
these types are first cousins from Scandinavia all the
way to Congo. The original Jews were, therefore,
short, dark people of the long headed type.

"The original Jew and Negro were, then, descended
from the same father. The evidence of intermarriage
you mention is a universal phenomenon, and the close
affinity between Hamitic and Semitic speech and between the Northern Hamitic people and the Semites,
shows close relationship, as you surmise.

"Anthropologists distinguish numerous types in
Africa, which you group together as Hamitic. I think
the term Hamitic should refer only to the Northern

ones, (part of the Mediterranean race) and have so
used the term.

"These are the conclusions to which I have come.
By the way, this same Mediterranean race, I find, has
survived in India where it had early percolated. The
Brachman caste seems to be very pure, but the lower
castes are more or less broad headed Asiatic aborigines.
Aryans are all gone, only their speech being left as evidence that they once conquered the land.

"It would be better to say that the Negro descended
from the Ancient Jewish type or Mediterranean race.
It is hardly correct, ethnically, to reverse the sentence."

ARTHUR T. ABERNETHY.

Rutherford College, N. C., February, 1910.

* Dr. Charles E. Woodruff.

The following table shows the principal nations which have descended from the ancient races:

I. ARYAN RACE	Persians, Hindoos, Greeks, Romans,	French, Italian, Spaniards, Portuguese,
	Celts,	Welsh, Irish, Highland Scots, Britons,
	Teutons,	Germans, Dutch, English, Swedes, Danes, Norwegians,
	*Slaves,	Russians, Poles, Bohemians,
II. SEMITIC RACE	Assyrians, Hebrews, Phoenicians,	
III. HAMITIC RACE	Chaldeans, Egyptians,	

Other authorities give as the children of Ham the people of Ethiopia, Babylonia, Egypt, The Colchians, Philistines, Lybians, Canaanites, Sidonians, and Phoenicians.

*The word "Slaves" originally meant "glorious," but came to have its present signification because at one time there were in Europe so many bondsmen of Slavonic birth.

THE JEW A NEGRO

DISCOVERY OF FIRE.

We learn from the profane history of Phoenicia, by Sanchoniatho, that, shortly after the flood, the art of generating fire was discovered by accidentally rubbing pieces of wood against each other. This enabled the sons of Noah to scatter about and to go into the mountains to live, as previous to this time, they were compelled to dwell in sections where tropical climates supplied them with food and bodily warmth.

The influence of this discovery on the civilization and development of humanity can hardly be estimated. Man originally lived in the tropics only. He knew nothing of clothing or artificial heat, ate none of the oily, heat-bearing substances such as meat, fish etc., and subsisted alone on fruit. His discovery of fire enabled him to eat fish and fowl, and with these, he could live anywhere. He could be independent of climate. As he found heat, he discovered he could eat many of the foods of the earth which he had not otherwise tried; animals were killed and cooked, and the art of treatment of various cooked foods was developed. As men found they could eat certain foods found in the woods by cooking them, they began to gather in places to cultivate these foods, hence we have cities, agriculture, society,

invention and commerce, directly due to fire. As men
lived together, they found residences were needed,
whence came our buildings. Then as they found they
could materially modify foods by cooking them, they
also tested fire on iron, steel, etc.,and thus discovered
the manufacture of steel and iron implements. This
made possible tools, and other implements, and with
these men learned of other inventions and conveniences,
by steadily improving those they utilized.

It was a step to discover that the application of personal attention to the growing grains improved their
quality and quantity, and when men discovered they
could make steel and iron pliable by heat, they shaped
plows and other instruments which they used for the
cultivation of the corn, wheat, and other products of
the fields, and this gave farms, and as they needed
more space, as the human family grew in numbers,
they cleared off the land, and communities of interest
brought farmers closer together until mutual societies
were formed, social intercourse resulted, and mutual
laws determined upon for protection and advantage.
Hence, from the savagery of original lawlessness to
the milder conditions of barbarity, and from that to civilization may be traced to the accidental discovery of
fire.

RACES OF MANKIND.

ONE OF AMERICA'S most reputable authorities says
that distinctions in form, color, and physiognomy

divide the human species into three great types, or races,
known as the Black (Ethiopian or Negro), the Yellow
(Turanian or Mongolian), and the white (Caucasian.)
These races subdivided themselves into numerous
families and peoples. We must not suppose each of
these three types to be sharply marked off from the
others: they shade into one another by insensible gradations. "Thus, passing from the temperate regions of
Northern Africa to the tropical countries of the interior of that continent, we find the different tribes
encountered exhibiting a 'chromatic scale' that em-
braces all the shades of color."

This is sufficient reply to those who claim the
superiority of the Jews to the Negroes because of their
occasional lighter color. We know that those race
characteristics to which we have referred, though capable of being greatly modified by climate and the varying
conditions of life, are very persistent. There has been
no perceptible change in the great types during historic times. The paintings upon the oldest Egyptian
monuments show us that at the dawn of history, about
five or six thousand years ago, the principal races
were as distinctly marked as now, each bearing its racial badge of color and physiognomy. As early as the
times of Jeremiah the permanency of physical characteristics had passed into the proverb: "Can the Ethiopian
change his skin?" On account of this persistent character of form, complexion and physiognomy, these physical distinctions form a better basis of classification than
language; for migrations and conquests often result in

people's giving up their own and adopting a foreign
tongue while at the same time retaining all their physical peculiarities. To efface these requires a great lapse of
time.   Thus, the Jews have in general adopted the language of the different peoples among whom they have
found a home; the Hebrew physiognomy is as marked
to-day as it was three thousand years ago.   The Author
uses almost the exact words of this celebrated authority.   There has been found a likeness in the Egyptian
and Jewish codes that has occasioned a comparison of
certain parts of the Egyptian "Book of the Dead,"lead-
ing great historians to the belief that Moses but copied
them bodily for his laws.   "There is certainly a very
close agreement," says Rawlinson, "between the moral
law of the Egyptians and the precepts of the Decalogue."

HOW THE JEWS WERE NAMED.

It might not be amiss to tell here how the Jews came
to be called Jews.   The reputed founder of the Jewish
race (as a race) was Abraham, the son of Terah, and
tenth in lineal descent from Noah to whom the right
of primo-geniture belonged.   The title of Jews was not
given them until after the Babylonish captivity, when
the tribe of Judah became the most considerable, and almost the whole of what was left of Israel.   The first
name that was given to Abraham and his children was
that of Hebrews which some derive from Heber, the
fifth in decent from Noah.   But it is hardly probable
that Abraham would call himself by his name, rather

than by that of any of his ten predecessors and the Author is of the opinion that it was given him by the Canaanites because he came thither from the other side of the Euphrates; the word Heber signifying in the original "the other side" whether of a river or any other thing. However, after Jacob had received the name Israel, they preferred that of Israelites to the name Hebrews.

WHO THE SEMITES ARE.

We must not confuse the word Semitic with the word Hebrew, used for a very small Semitic tribe which became isolated, or pocketed, on the Eastern Mediterranean shore and the interior valleys—a tribe which was very backward, being barbarous for thousands of years while great Semitic civilizations grew up in Egypt and around the Mediterranean and in Asia Minor. They even knew nothing of writing until the seventh century B. C. Nor should we mistake the word Jew, which now refers solely to that religion evolved about 600 B. C., by Ezra and the other Hebrews in their Babylonish captivity and after they were released by their conquerors. The Hebrew Jews were wonderful proselytes, and made converts in many other Semitic lands so that by the time of St. Paul they had synagogues in Egypt, Northern Africa, Spain, Italy, Greece and Asia Minor—indeed wherever Semites lived. Later, they proselyted among the Asiatic broad heads, and to such an extent that the present Jewish people are in most part descendants from Asiatic converts, while the Christian and Mohametan religions claim a great number of the Semites.

ORIGIN OF MAN AND THE FLOOD.

Many amusing conjectures are advanced respecting the location of the Garden of Eden. To anthropologists the chief interest lies in establishing the racial tendency of the first man. The Author is hardly ready to believe that the earth's surface was materially affected by the flood—to believe the entire face of nature was broken up, is ridiculous. Certainly there were changes wrought by the immense inundations, and time has doubtless covered the original Garden of Eden many fathoms deep beneath the dust and the sands of ages. But, whatever may be our individual views, it is hardly probable the Ark had floated very far away, (considering its dimensions and its having no method of propulsion) from the original site of its creation when the rains subsided, and the Ark rested on Mount Ararat. The fact that the dove was able to return to the Ark with the Olive branch proves conclusively that the earth had retained its usual physical conditions, minus, of course the great loss of carnal life which succumbed to the destructive elements. What we are most concerned to know, then, is not so much where the Garden of Eden was, as to what manner of man was the original inhabitant of the Garden of Eden and his sons down to Noah. Accepting the computations of almost all the earlier historians, there certainly were living in the time of Noah grandchildren of persons who had known Adam, and heard from our first father the story of the Garden of Eden. As letters had not been invented, and tradition was man's only history in those times, and since Noah survived the Deluge we are able to conduct traditional history carefully through the earlier development of the human family down to the bright era when writing was invented to preserve the doings of mankind. It would seem probable, then, that had there been any material change in nature wrought by the Deluge, or had the Garden of Eden been far remote from the resting spot of the Ark, Noah or his heirs would have remarked it. Noah was past 600 years old when he came from the Ark, and when we recognize the longevity of the antedeluvians, it is not improbable that he knew even some of the intimate family of Adam. Adam lived 930 years; Seth 912; Enos 905, Cainan 910; Mahalaleel 895; Jared 962; Enoch was translated at 365; Methuselah was 969, and Lamech, Noah's father, 777 years old. Nor let us think that these years were not equal with our present years in point of time, with the possible exception of four or five days. We know that the early method of computing time was siderial, and the old calendar as found by Caesar in Egypt was almost identical with our own.

It must be conceded that, taking into consideration the longevity of people in the antedeluvian days, there must have been, at the time of the flood, a great many more people on earth than even to-day as so many were born and so few died before arriving at ripe old age. When we know that mankind generally doubles itself about every 36 years, we are ready to agree with Mr. Whiston that the earth had, at the time of the Deluge, the enormous population of more than One Hundred Thousand Millions. For the benefit of those students of longevity who may wish to pursue this phase more deeply, the Author begs to introduce here the opinion of the ancient historians that the antedeluvian year was in absolute space of time nearly equal to our present and ancient lunar one, and only about ten days shorter, or to be precise, ten days, one hour and twenty-eight minutes and one-half shorter than our present solar year; yet it contained three hundred and sixty antedeluvian days, which were equal to only three hundred and fifty-five days, four hours, and about twenty minutes of our present days; the earth's diurnal motion having been retarded, and our days consequently lengthened in that proportion partly by the quanity of foreign matter derived from the comet at the Deluge, which God is believed to have sent to participate in the general physical upheaval which the earth underwent at that time. The Mosaic law distinguished four sorts of years:1. The civil, according to which all political matters were regulated, consisting of twelve solar, and afterwards lunar, months; 11. The sacred, which began in the month of Nisan, or March, which was the seventh of the civil year, and regulated the order of all their religious ceremonies; 111. The sabbatic, or seventh

/

THE JEW A NEGRO

year; and iv. The jubilee or 50th year, which was kept
at the end of seven weeks of years. It is plain by the
calculation which Moses gives of the days of the flood
(See Genesis, chapters 7 and 8 and elsewhere), that
the year consisted of three hundred and sixty-five
days, and consequently of twelve solar months,
the last of which consisted of thirty-five days. It
is probable, too, that Moses, having been brought up
in Egypt, had learned that way of reckoning from
them, because they are generally believed to have been
the first inventors of it. The Author does not agree
with Scaliger and others after him who suppose that
while this method of reckoning must have been that of
the Israelites, still they had an intercalary month
once in six score years, as the scriptures hint at no
such intercalation or year of thirteen months. In
Exodus 12:2 we find that Moses, by direct command of God, computed the years after that
period by moons. We know from Herodotus that
the Egyptians from their remarkable knowledge
of astronomy, which he credits them to have perfected,
adjusted the length of their year to the annual
revolution of the sun, by adding to their twelve months
of thirty days each five additional days and six hours,
while the Greeks and Romans used the more rude and
inconvenient form of lunar years, intercalating a
month every third year. In short, we have reason to
believe that but little difference has occurred in the
length of the year, and the only material changes in
the calendar may be credited to Caesar, with

Augustus' intervention in planning innovations in the computation of the Leap Year, and afterwards to Pope Gregory who made only slight modifications; none of these affecting the length of the actual year. But this digression is immaterial to the subject of this work.

Mr. Whiston believes that the air and general climatic conditions were different before the flood than after it, and the effects on human bodies as well as on the productions of the earth, but he thinks the purity and equality of the antedeluvian air were the natural and regular properties of an original earth such as one would rationally expect in a world newly come out of the hands of its creator and such as the generality of our fellow planets as far as we can observe are supposed to have had at first and hitherto retained. He supposes that a comet which he believes to have caused the Deluge (and God may have utilized this natural means of executing His Omnipotent Will) in passing by the earth, by its attraction accelerated the earth's annual motion and changed its then circular orbit into an ellipsis, and that the earth, at the Deluge, carried off vast quantities of the gross, heterogeneous and indigested masses with which the chaotic atmosphere of the comet was crowded, part of which were received into our air and the other part being mixed with the waters derived from the comet, settled and formed a new crust over the surface of the earth in some places. These two great changes in the natural world would have very considerable consequences. That made in the earth's orbit would, by placing us at a greater distance from the sun occasion a very sensible decrease in the heat of that luminary, which must, on calculation, have been a twenty-fifth part greater before the flood than since. (Whiston made this calculation) It is evident that the primo-genial soil would lie buried under the sediment (for the Author does not believe the substratum of the earth was changed. There is always a heavy sediment following protracted floods, even where no matter is supplied by atmospheric commotions such as the above mentioned comet) and Whiston believes the crust of the earth thus formed would be about five hundred and five feet thick, and it is reasonable that the fertile mold of the original earth would be much thinner spread in such sediment, and consequently with other things such as the dampening of the heats of the earth's centre, the earth after the Deluge could be nothing near so fruitful and luxuriant in her productions as the antedeluvian earth was. This supposition of a new earth acquired by the earth after the flood, may, by the way, also account for the phenomena of bones, teeth and shells of fish and other marine and vegetable productions so frequently dug up even on mountains and at great distances from the sea. The heterogeneous composition of our present gross atmosphere acquired likewise from the comet, must necessarily occasion great irregularities and depravations in the temperature and constitution of the air. For the difference of climates being not wholly due to the sun's heat or the nature of the air, but partly to those caloric and frigorific mixtures which are uncertainly contained therein, and our air being now, in the torrid zone, full of sulphureous and sultry, and in the frigid ones, of nitrous and freezing, effluvia or exhalations which may be removed on the veering of the winds from one region to another, those extremities of heat and cold and sudden changes of which we are now so sensible are thence easily accounted for, and we may very well credit our meteors, thunder, lightning, clouds, rain, winds and storms so common with us and of which the pure homogeneous antedeluvian air was perfectly free, to those same mixtures and exhalations. Thus we are fully convinced that the Deluge, while it may have wrought physiological and atmospheric changes, left no geographical differences on the earth, and that our first parents, being inhabitants of a perpetually tropical country in the land whence have emanated our dark races, and living to such advanced years, must have become, themselves, blacks, if climatic conditions alone were accountable for the nigrescence in mankind.

Before setting aside the subject of the creation of man, let us take some notice of the opinion of those who think that mankind was in being before Adam, who was the progenitor of the Jews only. To support this, they allege that Moses makes mention of two distinct creations, one of mankind in general, and the other of Adam and Eve (Gen. 1:27, and again Gen.2:7); and in the progress of his history gives strong intimations that there were several more men in the world when they were created; else it is not easily to be con-

ceived how Cain could be a tiller of the ground which
must presuppose all the articifers that have relation to
tillage; nor what reason he had to apprehend that every
one who found him would slay him; nor can his going
into another country, marrying a wife, and building a
city be otherwise accounted for. From which they would
infer that Moses intended only to give an account of the
origin of the Jews, and not of the primitive parents
of the whole human race. These objections are easily
answered, for the passage wherein the creation of man
is mentioned a second time is plainly no more than a
recapitulation of what had been said before of the creation of the world in general with a more particular de-
tail of that of our first parents. And as to the numbers
of men supposed to be in the world about the time of
the murder of Abel, it is by no means improbable that
these should be descendants of Adam and Eve whose
posterity in the space of near one hundred and thirty
years (for it was in that year of Adam's age that Seth
who was given in lieu of Abel was born) might, by
a fair calculation, be multiplied to many thousand
souls considering the primitive fecundity and that none
is supposed to have died in the interim.

But the most plausible objection to the Pre-Adam-
ites is that if Adam and Eve be allowed to be the pro-
genitors of all mankind there can be no tolerable cause
assigned of the difference in color between the whites
and blacks, it being very improbable that they were the
offspring of the same parents. To this it may be
answered that the variety of complexions in the world

may be rationally accounted for in another way. We know how the hair and color of men's bodies differ according to the climate they inhabit and their greater or lesser distance from the sun: we may therefore well conclude that the first colony which settled in a very hot country received a great change in their complexion proportionable to the heat of the climate, and became very tawny gradually inclining to blackness as the sun was more intense upon them. Hence in a generation or two that high degree of tawniness might become natural and at length the pride of the natives. The men might begin to value themselves upon this complexion, and the women to affect them the better for it, so that their love for their husbands and daily conversation with them might have a considerable influence upon the fruit of their wombs and make each child grow blacker and blacker, according to the fancy and imaginations of the mother; the force of which is evident from many instances. Upon this supposition the children thus produced must every birth approach nearer to an absolute blackness; and as their tender bodies came to be exposed naked (as the manner of such countries is) to the violent heat of the sun, their skin must needs be scorched in an extraordinary manner and perhaps its very texture altered, and by that means contract a blackness far superior to that of their parents. By such degrees it is not improbable that people of the fairest complexion when removed into a very hot climate may, in a few generations, become perfectly black. As to what some have imagined that this black-

ness was supernatural and a judgment inflicted upon
Ham, the son of Noah, for discovering his father's
nakedness and that all the people of that complexion
are the progeny of that undutiful son, this seems very
unlikely and without foundation, the curse on that occasion being laid on Canaan, the son of Ham, by name,
and yet his posterity are allowed not to have been black.
If we admit that Ham's posterity were the blacks we
must take into consideration two features of the Hamitic and Semitic life which gives us the reason for finding
in the modern Jews the *features* with a much less
coloring of the Africans. History shows that the
Jews, while always a migratory race, spent their first
years in Egypt and other parts of Africa, many being
born there, and, as the Author shows in this work,
many the inter-bred descendants of the Hamitic and
Semitic families. The Hamitic races, having remained
stationary in Egypt, as history shows, continued as
the survivals of the fittest for that region, to grow more
and more black, while their Jewish brothers, removing
into less tropical zones, in time lost some of their tawniness and grew more and more into the appearance of
the white man. But no climatic transmigration could
remove the facial, aye, and other characteristics peculiar to those two peoples.

CURSE OF HAM.

When Noah was acquainted with the irreverent action of Ham, he cursed him in a branch of his posterity: "Cursed," said he, "Be Canaan, a servant of servants shall he be unto his brethern." (Gen. 9: 25) This curse, if it be a curse, being pronounced not against Ham, the immediate transgressor, but against his son, who does not appear from the words of Moses to have been in any way concerned in the crime (though the Jews believe it was Canaan who first discovered his father's nakedness and went and told his father who made sport of the accident) has occasioned several conjectures: some have believed that Noah cursed Canaan because he could not have well cursed Ham himself whom God not long before had blessed. Other authorities claim that this curse was merely a prophecy that the sons of Japhet and Shem should have dominion over the sons of Ham. A learned author has affirmed (See Mede's Works) that there has never yet been a son of Ham who has shaken a sceptre over the head of Japhet; Shem has subdued Japhet, and Japhet has subdued Shem, but Ham never subdued either.

However, this must be a mistake, if there be any truth in what the Egyptian histories relate of the actions of Sesostris and some others of their Kings who have conquered the greatest part of Asia and Europe and consequently may be said to have subdued both. Besides, we find the Israelites were long the slaves of

Mizraim, or the Egyptians; and we see no reason why the shameful submission which Rehoboam, the son and successor of Solomon made to Shishak, the Egyptian Pharoah who, after taking all the strong cities of Judah seems to have had Jerusalem delivered up to him without opposition to be spoiled with the temple, may not be deemed a servitude, it being expressly said that the Jews should be his servants. Ham also appears to have encroached upon Shem very early for he seems to have driven the Shemites out of their first seats in Shinaar, and everybody knows the Babylonians who were Hamites had a considerable share in the destruction of the Assyrian empire. But a stronger instance than any of the preceeding is the Babylonish captivity in which the Jews themselves were the sufferers. Indeed, the very branch of Canaan seems to have had great success against Japhet not only by the exploits of the Carthaginians (originally Canaanites) in Italy, but by their conquest in Spain.

WHERE HAM WENT AFTER THE DELUGE.

Ham probably removed from Shinaar. Supposing him to be the Cronus of Sanchoniatho, he reigned in Phoenicia. According to others who make him to be the same with Menes, he must have settled in Egypt, which indeed in Scripture is often called the land of Ham. Cush, his eldest son, according to Josephus and the ancients, was the father of the Ethiopians who, he

says, were in his time called Cusheans not only by themselves but all Asia over.　But it is not likely that if
Mizraim and Canaan settled themselves in the land
between him and Shinaar that his son Nimrod would
be found erecting a monarchy so early in that country.
It is more probable that he seated himself in the South-
eastern part of Babylonia and in the adjoining part of
Susiana still called Khuzestan or the country of Chuz;
from whence his posterity in the succeeding generations might have passed into other countries.　That
part of Arabia near the Red Sea was named Cush appears from Scripture.　Cushan and Midian are joined
together as one or neighboring people dwelling in tents,
and in another place the Arabs are made to border on
the Cushites, which, therefore cannot be the Ethiopians; to which may be added other Scriptural proofs;
in a word, by Cush in Scriptures is always to be un-
derstood Arabia.　As for those texts which are alleged
to prove Cush is sometimes taken to mean Ethiopia,
they may also be expounded of Arabia.　Cush, according to the Arab and Persian traditions which name him
Cuth, was King of the territory of Babel and resided
in Erak　where there　were two　cities of his　name,
whence, among other reasons, Dr. Hyde is of the opinion that Cush reigned in Babylonia and that his descendants removed into Arabia.　This has given occasion to those who suppose Cush to be Ethiopia to
spread them all along the coast of Africa to the end of
Mauritania.　Those who place them in Arabia are divided about their situations.　To follow, there-

fore, the rules we have laid down, we will suppose (1st) That Seba situated himself somewhere in the South of Chaldea or the Arabia Erak, because (2nd) his second brother Havilaha's country lay there-abouts, watered by the Pison. (3rd) Sabtah's seat perhaps lay more to the South where we find a city called Saphtha by Ptolemy not far from the Persian gulf and another named Sabatha, lower down in Arabia Felix which comes much nearer Sabtah. (4th) Raamah or Rhegma may find a place more Southward still, about a city called Rhegama by Ptolemy in the same gulf. Some moderns mention a city not far from it called Baden which Dr. Wells does not doubt was the residence of his son Dedan. Though others will have Raamah and both his sons, Sheba as well as Dedan, to people the parts adjacent to the Red Sea. They conclude Dedan to have been near Edom because Ezekiel joins them together; as Raamah must have been near Sheba, being mentioned as joint traders to Tyre in spices, by the same prophet, (Ezekiel 27:22); and elsewhere Sheba or Seba are joined as neighbors though distinguished as different kingdoms. They seem to have possessed a larger part of Arabia, for Pliny observes that the Sabean nations inhabited from sea to sea; i. e. from the Arabian to the Persian gulf. A late writer supposes Sheba lived on the borders of the land of Midian, and gave name to the country whose queen in after ages went to visit Solomon. But the Arabs say the country of Sheba lies a great way more to the South in Yaman, or, as we call it, Arabia Felix

near the Indian Sea, the chief city of which was formerly Saba now called Nared. And it must be confessed
this seems to be the country of Sheba mentioned in
Scripture for frankincense grows thereabouts. (5th)
Sabtecha has puzzled all the geographers to assign his
quarters. Bochart, not finding a place in Arabia
which bore any resemblance to the name, passes over to
Carmania in Persia and presses the city Samydace into
the service, observing that M. and B. are often changed, the one for the other, by the Arabs and their neighbors; on the other hand, Dr. Wells imagines that the
Saracens are the descendants of Sabtecha which nation
being styled at first by the Greek Sabtacena, that name
was afterward softened into Saracena; and the rather,
he thinks, because alluding to the Arabic verb Saraka,
to steal, it served for a nickname. Though indeed the
word Saraceni is no other than Shark in which in Arabic signifies Easterlings; as the African Arabs west of
Egypt are called Mograbins or Westerlings. (6th)
Nimrod is agreed to have kept possession of Shinaar
and erected a kingdom there making Babel the seat
of his empire. Mizraim stands in the place of the
second son of Ham; for there is a great dispute whether
this is the name of a single person or a people as having a dual termination; though the verb in the text
where he is said to beget Ludin is in the singular number which favors the former opinion. It is plain that
the names of Ludin and all the rest of his descendants
are plural.

As to the nations descended from Mizraim: First,

the Ludim are judged to be the people above Egypt called by the Greeks Ethiopians, and at present Abyssins.
Bochart endeavors to prove it by no less than ten arguments. We rarely hear them called otherwise in
Scripture than Lud, either from the name of their
founder or their country. In one passage of Scripture
Lud are called a *mixed people;* in others they are said
to be very skillful in drawing the bow which the Ethiopians are famous for; and in two of the above mentioned passages Lud is joined with Cush and Phut, as
are the Ludins elsewhere with the Egyptians, from
which it may be inferred they were all neighboring people. The Anamim are thought by Bochart to be the
Ammonians of inhabitants of that part of Lybia where
stood the temple of Jupiter Ammon, descended, according to Herodotus, partly from the Egyptians and partly
from the Ethiopians.

The Lehabim are supposed to be the same with the
Ludim who, with the Sukkims and Cushites, came out
of Mizraim, or Egypt, with Shishak, to invade Judea;
these therefore, may not improbably be judged to be
the Libyans of Cyrenaica, or Proper Libya, in Egypt.

And thus the Author might speak of the settlements
affected by the Napthuhim, Pathrusim, Cashluhim,
Philistim (whom we know to have first settled Egypt
before going into Canaan) Caphtorim. etc.

Authors are not agreed about the country where
Phut, the third son of Ham, settled himself. Bochart
says that Mizraim and Phut divided Africa between
them. We find Cush, Lud and Phut among *the*

*nations, who, according to Jeremiah's prophecy, were
to overrun Egypt,* as Nebuchadnezzar afterwards did;
which looks as if Phut's quarters lay somewhere between Cush and Babylon.

The posterity of Canaan viz: Sidon, Heth, the
Jebusites, Amorites, Girgashites, Hivites, Arkites,
Simites, Arvadites, Zermarites, and Hamathites, undoubtedly settled in Phoenica. This last statement
should be well borne in mind in considering the table
given at the first of this book.

BEGINNING OF MANKIND.

It is impossible to know the *source* of the human race,
since the spot of creation and the Garden of Eden is
shrouded in mystery, and doubt. If we accept the
scholarly view of the greatest historians of Europe who
studied this matter under the tutelage of the great
Duke of Marlborough in the fifteenth century, we find
the most probable location of the Garden of Eden at the
junction of the Euphrates and Tigris rivers. If we
knew positively of what terrestrial section Adam was
an inhabitant, it would be easier to ascertain the original physical attributes and relationships of the human
race, and hence whether he were a Negro or a
man of white skin. We do know that the description of his clothing indicates that Adam lived
in a tropical country, and to believe that *all* the
insects, animals and creatures of animal life in existence
to-day were represented either in Eden or pre-

served of their kind in the Ark is preposterous. They have, many of them, been evolved by the processes of inter-generation and "crossing" just as we to-day are able to create new kinds of flowers, plants, and the like. (See the references to the first cooked food, elsewhere in this work). This would indicate that mankind orginally dwelt in the tropics where fruits were plentiful and no requirements of warmth to the body were essential.

But we are more concerned about the positive creation of the different races *after* the Deluge, if we are to accept the Mosaic account as correct. This seems to us the most plausible, aside from any claims to its inspiration. The Author has seen fit elsewhere to introduce a very extended account of the Deluge in order to set forth what he believes to be the most natural evidences of all that is claimed in the Mosaic accounts. We are positively assured from the acount of the Deluge that the human race had its second beginning in this survival of Noah and his three sons. It would require volumes upon volumes to enter upon any scientific dissertation upon the various interchanges to which mankind may have been subjected until we have reached our present remarkable condition of humanity in which we find—from the same *original head,* the sole man Noah—so many differing species of man. While we may offer scholarly excuses for pigmentations that make one man black and another brown, and still another yellow and yet another white, we are at loss to account for any extraneous influences which could perpetrate or effect such directly racial peculiarities as are visible in the almond eyes of the Chinese, the curly hair of the Negro, the straight hair of the Chinaman, both of whom have undergone very nearly similar atmospheric and physical exposures. Besides, it must be plainly denied—and repudiated as demonstrated fact to the contrary—that climate is *entirely* responsible for the fact of the Negro's darkness or the Caucasian's blondness. It has been clearly shown that the Negro who has not intermarried has retained his intense darkness even in the temperate zones, and the best refutation of this old time theory is found in the Esquimo who, although for at least five hundred years' resident in the Arctic region, and that where the sun only shines six months during a full year, still remains black.

Since we cannot lay it to climatic or local conditions, we are then forced to reach our conclusions through an impartial study of the *physical* similarities of races; for, should we permit ourselves to be guided to our conclusions by other judgments, we will be met with contradictions in physical life in these localities which will lead us entirely into the dark.

A study of the monuments and other delineations of ancient personages clearly demonstrates that the thick lip, peculiar bone formations, and general similarities found in nationalities (but peculiar to certain races alone) are *not* matters of locality but of racial relationship. An instance of this is peculiarly demonstrated in the descendants of certain Mongolian missionaries who, according to the imperial records of China, were sent to what is now known to the American continent and perfected settlements long before our permanent establishment of sovereignty in the United States. Many centuries after these religious invasions, we are told that tribes have been found in Alaska, where these missionaries made their first pilgrimages, possessing the peculiar characteristics of the Mongolians to a marked degree. Yet location has in this instance been entirely distinct and unsimilar. Let us take the case of Cleopatra— accredited by history as the most gorgeous and lovely of womanhood. Dark, of Graeco-Egyptian blood, she was assuredly Negro for we find she possessed the thick sensual lips, the other unfailing hand marks of the African, while her features indicate an infusion of Jewish blood and her conduct in her political life showed an unsual affinity with the Hebrews. We will have occasion to speak of Cleopatra at greater length further on in this work.

From pictures made three thousand years ago in Egypt, the differences of racial characteristics were very clearly depicted in the hair, the features of the face, and indeed, the color of the skin. When, considered by this ethnological standard we note the fact that the Anglo-American (Caucasian), with his brown hair, his fair face, high, prominent and broad forehead, his great brain capacity, his long head and his delicately moulded features, bears such a marked contrast to the Chinaman with his yellow skin, flat nose, black, coarse hair, almond-shaped eyes, and round skull, and we are brought face to face with the fact that the best authorities believe that it has required thousands of years to evolve these racial differences from one original species (The Egyptians held at the time of Herodotus, about 450 B. C., that man had been in existence twenty-five thousand years) we are forced to recognize the still remaining strikingly similar racial characteristics of the Jewish and Negro types in their eyes, hair, forehead, thick, sensual lips—and the peculiar formations of their finger nails, and we wonder at the little differences wrought in all those long periods, notwithstanding the migrations of the Hebrew race. Studies of Jew and Negro portraits tell their own story best. They have been selected from Negroes and Jews of the higher order, and without regard to location of the subject selected. The Author regards the best specimens of Negro and Jew types from European and African countries, but being unwilling to compare any other than portraits of those whom he has been permitted to personally interview for the purpose of re-assuring himself as to nationalities, he is forced to content himself with pictures of only American subjects. It is not amiss just here to introduce a feature in the earliest attempts at Central American civilization, which, the Author believes, has its bearing on this subject. Our ethnologists have remarked the striking similarity between the resemblance of Toltec and Egyptian civilization. In art, architecture and industry, in worship, and the elements of knowledge they are a resemblance to Egyptian models. Let us add to this the still more remarkable claim of some reputable ethnologists that the Esquimo tribes found in North America have many traits in their language, habits and physical features resembling the Hebrews; and couple to this statement the claim of other historians and ethnologists that they were probably a remnant of the ten lost tribes of Israel. Noting the apparent similarity of these Egyptian inhabitants of Central America (The Toltecs) with their already recognized racial intermixture with the Hebrews; considering the resemblance of the Esquimox mentioned above, when we note the unquestionable Negro features of the Esquimox, we at once have a further proof of the contention claimed by this book. The arguments set forth by Hebrew writers that their race has been kept aloof from intermarriages by Divine interference, falls flat in the face of uncontrovertible historical proofs, and the well known Jewish proclivity to over-ride even the directly delivered admonitions of God as did the Jews on so many occasions expressly chronicled in their history. It is not reasonable that a race so callous to direct Divine guardianship in matters affecting their personal welfare, would preserve inviolate an order to abstain from the exercises of a passion so characteristic of the Hebrew blood as that of cohabitation. Besides, we need no conjecture on this point; their history is conclusive to the contrary.

LANGUAGE A TEST OF RELA-TIONSHIP.

Many anthropologists base their deductions on racial affinities on the similarity or dissimilarity of languages or dialects employed by these races. The sons of Shem Ham and Japhet all took part in the building of the tower of Babel, and if we may judge by the fact that in the confusion of tongues administered as a rebuke to the builders, it is noticeable that the *Canaanites* (descendants of Ham) and the *Hebrews afterwards retained the same language.* If Leo and the African historians are to be credited, Sabtecha, the son of Cush, first peopled the Sahara between the mountains of Atlas and Nigritia, and therefore probably Nigritia itself. From the same author it appears, that the various Nigritian dialects bear an affinity to the Chaldee, Arabic and Egyptian tongues, to which we may add, and consequently to the Ethiopic which does not differ widely from them. One historian of note says, in speaking of the Nigritiae and their affiliations with the Carthagenians and Egyptians: "One part of the armies of the Carthaginians consisted of Nigritian troops. They used scythed chariots in their wars and were armed after the manner of the western Ethiopians, with bows and arrows of the same make." This same author then plunges into an extensive anthropological account, and concludes with the statement: "This evinces that the Negroes, or blacks, held an early correspondence with the ancient

Mauritanians, Numidians, and Carthaginians."

Taking a part of Africa as an object for consideration, in a country of so vast an extent as Ethiopia, inhabited by various nations, it is natural to suppose that
no small variety of languages, at least of dialects, must
have prevailed. The most ancient of these was undoubtedly that called the Ethiopic into which the Holy
Scripture was formerly translated, and in which all the
books of the Abassines both sacred and profane are
written. Some authors have informed us that this
language nearly resembles the Chaldee, but according
to Ludolphus *who spent over sixty years in the study
of it,* it bears as great an affinity to the Hebrew and
Syriac and approaches nearer still to the Arabic from
which, to him, it seems immediately to be derived. In
short, there is so perfect an agreement between them
that whoever understands the one may, without any
difficulty, make himself master of the others; he even
goes so far as to assert that a competent knowledge of
the Hebrew will enable a student soon to make a very
laudable progress in the Ethiopic. To support this view,
we know that the Ethiopians received an accession
of almost half a million Egyptians under the reign of
Psammitichus (according to Herodotus). Many of
these had acted in military capacity in different parts
of Ethiopia for three years, when they had deserted *to*
the King of Ethiopia and become citizens of his country. These were given lands by the king, and became a
part of his government, and people. Africanus, the

historian, declares the Ethiopians were masters in Egypt 80 years before the time of Psammitichus.

Herodotus shows that the origin of the alphabet was Phoenician, (Semitic) as does Pliny, and taken directly from the Egyptian forms, as Eusebius and the classic authorities from Plato to Tacitus agree. The Phoenicians (Jews) were great travelers, aptly called "colossal pedlars of the old world" by Dr, Huxley. Thus we have a connecting link here further proving their early relationship.

Accepting the table given elsewhere in this work as a correct division of the races, we find the Old Testament filled with Egyptian words in the Semitic form, and we know that the Jews grew from a race of only seventeen souls to over three millions of people in Egypt. It is seen that the *Phoenicians* as well as the Assyrians were in part members of the Hebrew (Semitic) family. It is elsewhere shown that the Phoenicians were pioneer settlers among almost all the other races, and intermarried indiscriminately with them. Their blending with the Egyptian (Hamitic) people is a part of history's record. The Hebrew alphabet was, of itself, of Egyptian origin; their language, customs and education were of Egyptian origin, and it is a surprising fact that many of the *identical* Symbols of Egyptian ideograms were found even among the earlier races of the Mexicans.

PRO—EGYPTIAN JEWISH TENDENCY.

Herodotus (l. i i) affirms that the Ammonii were originally a colony of Egyptians and Ethiopians; and that they spoke a language composed of words from both those nations. It is elsewhere shown that the Jews and Egyptians had intermarried; here we have another instance of the Egyptians in turn being interwed to the Ethiopians.

There seems everywhere in Jewish history a pro-Egyptian tendency. This is remarkably apparent by the readiness with which they lapsed into the idolatrous worship of Egypt, especially under the very shadow of Sinai; Moses had scarce made Aaron High Priest when, under the very sound of God's omnipotent voice during the hours when Moses was receiving the Decalogue from God's own hands, Aaron began to busy himself to set up the Golden Calf in the valley, and engaged the waiting Hebrews in its general worship. So "Egyptianized" had the Jews become in Moses' time that even while he was receiving the ten commandments from the hands of God in the mountain, the Jews with Moses' brother, were worshiping an Egyptian idol—the Golden Calf----just below the mountain. And just here it is well to note that such eminent writers as Suidas in his Sarapis, Rutin in his ecclesiastical history, Peirrerius in his heiroglyphics, Hottinger and others, all seemed to believe that the very origin of the worship of the Calf by the people of Egypt was introduced as an honor to Joseph (the Jew) in memory of the seven cows which represented the plenty by which he preserved that country from perishing; and this seems the most probable because several of the most ancient authors besides those above quoted, agree that this cow or ox (Apis) was represented carrying a bushel upon its head which might be designed to signify the plenty of corn which that patriarch caused to be laid up.

Even Solomon with all his wisdom returned to the idolatry of the Egyptians; the father of Abraham was guilty of it, and *at one time* ten of the twelve tribes of Israel revolted in a body, notwithstanding all their divine tuition, and re-established the methods of Egyptian worship among themselves.

Ptolemy Soter, the first Ptolemy, had imported one million Jews and by coarse and indiscriminate inter-marriages for over three hundred years, we find such an Egyptianized-Hebrew mixture that in one of their queens celebrated for her beauty, Cleopatra, there was a splendid "blend" of the Egyptian luxuriousness and the incomparable Hebrew possibilities of provoking sensuality. After Ptolemy VI. there was, as we know, a break in the Egyptian line and an indiscriminate and irregular form of government which came again into the garish light by the illuminating festivities of this beautiful Cleopatra, daughter of Aules. Plutarch denies that she was so beautiful, but declares that she possessed the art of wit and entertainment to perfection. The principal generals and soldiers of Cleopatra were Jews, and Ananias the Jew was one of her head generals. Cleopatra's pro-Jewish sentiments are remarked in history. With all her possessions her prevailing ambition was to be known as mistress of Judea. She begged this of Alexander, and later of Herod, and finally of Anthony, that splendid, genial souled prince of sunshine who was the most magnificent specimen of manhood Rome ever produced and whose heart was too magnanimous for his head. Anthony could not withstand the delicate coquetries of this histrionic genius, and he gave over to Cleopatra absolutely the Sovereignty of Jericho, the richest, pleasantest and most fertile of all the territory of Judea.

Of the Philistines, we know, too, that they were from the loins of Mizraim (Hamitic) and that Egypt was their first seat. The tendency of the Jews to mingle with them in matrimony when not too carefully pressed by their law givers is well attested in the Bible.

A further suggestion of this tendency is the fact that the language of the Ethiopians and Jews *remained the same* after the division of the tongues at Babel; and we have elsewhere been told that the Egyptians got their learning and their language from the Ethiopians. Ethiopia and Egypt united under Actisanes, King of Egypt.

Herodotus infers that the Hebrews, when they were originally a colony of the Egyptians derived the rite of circumcision from the Egyptians, and consequently

agreed with them in all their customs and manners.
(See Herodotus Book 2, Chapters 36 and 37.)
They also practiced embalming like the Egyptians.
The Egyptians also refused to eat hog meat, and the
Jews are said to have copied that custom from them.

INTERMARRIAGE INDUBITABLE PROOF.

We are forced to acknowledge the most indubitable evidences of racial relationship to be those of intermarriage as is stated elsewhere in this work. Language
alone may not always be conclusive. The Jews have
ever been a prolific as well as a nomadic people, and
their gravest offense seems to have been that of disregard for the divine purpose of retention of their kind
among itself. A celebrated English authority on this
subject terms intermarriage "the crying abuse of the
ancient Jews." On this subject the Jews have always
feigned considerable indignation at any intimation that
their race is not the most exclusive and selfcontained
in the world, claiming it to have been kept so through
all history by divine dispensation. But they fail to recognize the historic fact that their leaders, both in
their military, political and religious life, for the most
part openly disregarded any such divine interference and
married outside their own race at will. The Author is
unable to comprehend how the Jews may consistently
lay claim to racial self-retention, in face of even their
law of Moses which admitted the Egyptians in the

third generation into the Jewish congregation and full rights of citizenship. (Duet. 23:07). A long list of questions was put to those desirous of admission into "the congregation of the Lord" as Moses termed it (and we must remember that at this time Israel was a theocracy, and admission to the church privileges included all the privileges of ordinary citizenship). The Edomites and Egyptians *were received under a special providence of God* "because Israel had been a stranger in Egypt." One especially flagrant misuse of the earlier intention that the Jews should preserve the blood inviolate is found in the fact that although the Moabites and Ammonites were not to be admitted even after the tenth generation (for this is the exact letter of the text which we falsely translate "until after the tenth generation") we find Boaz, the greatgrandfather of David (and certainly therefore of the tribe of Judah) married to Ruth the Moabitess. The apology for this reckless intermarriage practice is of itself, a strong argument for the contention of the Author who only deems it necessary to demonstrate by proofs that the Jews are and were of a mongrel ancestry. They claim that as the text uses the words in Moses *in the masculine only* no restrictions were to be placed in the selection of their women. This seems to have been the view of their principal heads ·since most of them put that view into practice by intermarriage at will.

There was an express command of God that if any stranger was desirous of being admitted to eat of the

passover, he was first to be circumcised after which he
was to be admitted, not only to that grand solemnity
but also to all the other religious privileges in common with the Israelites. Of this number was the great
part of the mixed multitude which came with them out
of Egypt, and of the conquered inhabitants of Canaan.
"And indeed," says one historian, "the condition of
those who became circumcised was so preferable to that
of those who continued in their old religion that the
number of them increased very much and this is supposed to have put the selfish Jews upon the distinction
between proselytes of the gate and proselytes of
righteousness; the former of which, continuing uncir-
cumcised and being bound to observe only the precepts
of Noah, were kept in a state not many degrees better
than slavery." We find no less than one hundred and
fifty-three thousands and upwards of this kind in Solomon's time, and the Jews profited by this sale of privileges to take into their number hundreds of thousands. The first sort were, it is true, not permitted to
live among the Jews in marital relations, but history
proves that they became extremely remiss and negligent
in this respect and were often reproved by the prophets
for it. However, reproof will not eradicate the fact of
hybrid offspring.

The profligate intermarriages of the Jews were not
confined to the common people, but even priests, levites,
and heads of families had made with some of their idolatrous neighbors such domestic alliances that in the

time of Ezra they had introduced a mixed mongrel
breed of Egyptians, Moabites, Ammonites, Samaritans
and other strange nations among the true Israelites,
and Ezra compelled a general census and an oath that
they should put away their *strange wives and children.*
As many on this occasion confessed to having had children by these strange wives, does it not follow that these
practices, no matter how rigid after-laws may have been
enforced, set adrift on earth another mongrel nonde-
script type of humanity masquerading as Jews? But
these instances are only a few out of thousands known
to history. The Jews seem to have a fascination for
going after strange gods —and strange women. *In
the very outset of Israel* we are told that "it was the one
dread of Rebeckah that Jacob might take a daughter
of Heth to wife."

LOOSENESS OF MARRIAGE LAWS OF JEWS.

That the Jews accommodated their marriage con-
tracts to their loose ideas of intermarriage even to the
very advent of Jesus is evident from history. "If any
one," said the Rabbis, "see a woman handsomer than
his wife, he may dismiss his wife and marry that
woman," and they had the audacity to justify it by a
text of Scripture. Even the strict Shammai held that
if a wife went out without being shrouded in a veil
which eastern women still wear, she might be divorced,

and hence many Rabbis locked up their wives when
they went out! While some held that divorce should
be lawful only for adultery, others, like Josephus, claimed the right to send away their wives if they were not
pleased with their behavior. The school of Hillel even
maintained that if a wife cooked her husband's food
badly by oversalting or overroasting it, he might put
her away, and he might also do so if she were stricken
by any grievous bodily afflictions. The facility of divorce among the Jews had indeed become so great a
scandal even among their heathen neighbors that the
Rabbis were fain to boast of it as a privilege granted
to Israel and not to other nations.

EARLIEST INSTANCES OF INTERMARRIAGE.

The beginning of mankind, as we have already stated, was from three men, Shem, Ham and Japhet. We
have learned from Genesis 11:2, that they traveled from
the East and settled in a plain in the land of Shinaar.
We know from Scriptures that Abraham went into
Canaan about five years after Ham's death, if we accept
the usual chronology, for it is believed Ham lived about
450 years. Let us not forget that the Jews of the one
clan— those who hold to the prophecies—— claim their
descent directly from Abraham. Any evidence of intermarriage traceable to Abraham's family or his immediate posterity has direct bearing on this contention.
What are the historic facts? Abraham was the son of

Terah, who is mentioned in Genesis as a descendant of Shem, and was born in Ur of the Chaldees, who, we have already learned, were doubtless Hamitic, and we know from Genesis that the ancestors of Abraham had dwelt for many centuries in the land of the Chaldees. Terah, Abraham's father, had been a worshiper of idols, and —what is more important—the people of Mesopotamia are referred to by Jehovah as "thy brethren" when the call was given to Abraham to get him out of Haran where his father had died. Abraham's father, Terah, was the son-in-law of Nimrod, according to the eastern authors; this would give us added proof of the direct descent of Abraham himself from Negro ancestry.

Let this fact be further borne in mind: It was in the lower part of the Tigris Euphrates valley the Semitic family mingled with the people already in possession of the soil, and formed a mixed people known as the Chaldeans, and it was from the land of the Chaldees Abraham was born.

Let us take the case of Moses by whom the laws against intermarriage were directly delivered, and from whom, if any one, we would rationally expect the most conclusive testimony as to the correct application of the law. That Moses lived on terms of the closest social intimacy with the Egyptians is assured by the manner in which he conversed with Pharoah, and indeed by the very fact of his discovery and adoption by the daughter of Pharoah just after his birth. We have learned that

Abraham had lived in Chaldea! we know that Nitocris
and Sesostris, queen and king of Egypt were Ethiopians (Hamitic) and certainly Negroes; and it was
when Joseph was ruler under the earlier Pharoah that
he sent for his brethern and settled them in Egypt.
This self-same Ethiopian king, Sesostris, was the greatest of all the Egyptian monarchs, and under him the
Jewish population in Egypt had increased until it was
more than three millions of people. The objection to
this rapid increase occasioned the exodus of the Jews
from Egypt after Joseph's death. *We find the direct
descendant of this Ethiopian king (a Negro, the daughter of a Pharoah) adopting Moses,* and Genesis says:
"He became her son" which would clearly indicate a
close social intercourse between the Ethiopians and the
Jews.

Yet, as soon as we find Moses at marriageable age he
fled into the land of the Ethiopian, and married Zipporah, a native of Cush. That Zipporah was black is
proved by the original Hebrew version of the Bible
where in that part of Jeremiah the prophet is made to
exclaim: "Can the Ethiopian change his skin?" we find
the word "Cushite" instead of "Ethiopian." And, in
the book of Isaiah, we find Egypt, Patros, and Cush
joined together, and consequently Cush is taken for
Ethiopia. But the original speaks for itself: The Old
Testament, in Numbers 12:1, says: "And Miriam and
Aaron spoke against Moses *because of the Ethiopian
woman whom he had married; for he had married an*

Ethiopian woman." That this complaint was not occasioned by any *unusualness* of this marriage to the Ethiopian is proved by further reading of the original which sets forth as a reason for this complaint that Moses had won the woman's affections because of his God's having conversed in person with him, and the probable fact of Zipporah's boasting of Moses' superiority over other men on that account.

We must agree with the deliberate decision of the Scriptures as shown by its geographical and political references that Cush, the eldest son of Ham, was the great progenitor of the Ethiopians; and such being the fact as clearly shown, Moses took to wife a woman of Negro blood.

The Author feels it not amiss, just here, to introduce some material regarding these Ethiopians, although in another section of the book their history is ethnically considered more at length. The Ethiopians were superior to the Egyptians in point of antiquity, since Cush, their great ancestor, was the eldest son of Ham, and Diodorus Siculus says that they claim to have been the *first* nation to have a religion established. Homer himself seems to countenance this when he introduces Jupiter attended by other gods as present at an anniversary sacrifice or grand entertainment prepared for him by the Ethiopians. The Jews claimed Arabians as the descendants of Abraham through Eber, but Herodotus and Xenophon both declare them Ethiopians. Pliny asserts that the Ethiopians were masters of Egypt

before the Trojan war, and declares that they practiced
circumcision and had many other similar customs as
known to the Jews and Egyptians. Aristeus, Philo and
Polyhistor all three declare that Job married one of
these Arabian Ethiopian types. The learned Oriental-
ist, Professor Morris Jastrow, of the University of
Pennsylvania, says the three friends of Job were Arabians.

The Author believes that the relationship between the
Jews and the Egyptians is so clearly demonstrated in
the instances of Joseph and his posterity that it was recognized. Considering these facts, it is probable that
Moses in his triumphal military excursions against the
Ethiopians, was courted and wed by Tharbis, the
daughter of the King of Ethiopia, out of respect for
the great law-giver's military renown and splendor. It
seems hardly probable that, had not Moses been of
similar caste, i. e. of Negro blood, he would have wed-
ded himself to an Ethiopian. Josephus and other historians give credence to the statement that the wife
of Moses was this princess Tharbis.

From the accepted Biblical account we are forced to
accept the conclusion that the entire plan of judicature
set forth by Moses for the Hebrews was arranged and
advised by Jethro, his father-in-law, who was a Cushite. (Exodus 18:14). A peculiar co-incidence is found
by the reading of an old inscription, regarding Sargon,
the Semitic King of Agade. He was the offspring of the
blended races of upper Chaldea and the Semitic tribes

which arrived later, and was known as the Chaldean
Moses. Abraham's intermarriage with Hagar shows
an early social (if not physical and racial) relationship
between the Negroes and the Jews, for Hagar was an
Ethiopian. Yet she was accepted into the domestic
circle with the Jewish wife of Abraham, and bore offspring to him, as we are told by the Scriptures. We
must not forget, also, that it was by the direct advice of
Abraham's wife that this offspring was begotten of Hagar, who, being barren herself, counselled Abraham
to beget his long-promised offspring from Hagar, and
they both looked to this intercourse to produce the long
expected descendancy assured Abraham. Surely, if
Abraham had not been himself Negro, he would not
have been so ready to tinge an assured posterity whose
certainty God had pledged in His own good time, with
the tawniness of Ethiopia!

The next important intermarital event in the Jewish
early epoch of which history speaks is that of Joseph,
although we must not regard these as the solitary instances of such inter-wedlock. They serve to estab-
lish the proofs of the relationship which existed between the Jews and that nation which we now know to
have been Negro, and determine the contention of the
Author by irrefutable proofs. Joseph is regarded by
many as the real starting point of Jewish history in its
relation to the Messianic prophecy. He was, we know,
the most prominent of the sons of Israel (Jacob).
Pharoah, in his endeavor to honor Joseph, *gave him the*

*daughter of the Priest of On, Potipherah, an Egyptian,
to wife.* From this relationship two sons were born
to Joseph. The reader must not lose sight of the fact,
elsewhere herein historically proved, that it was no
less a repugnance to the white races to intermarry with
the black races than it was to the blacks to take white
consorts, as they considered white people in common
with the devil and thus painted all their symbols of the
wicked one. If Joseph had not been of identical or
relative color with the Egyptians, it is not probable he
would have considered this connection with Potipherah
as an honorable or desirable one; however, even ad-
mitting this may not have been the case, the intermarriage established a racial relationship *beginning at that
time.* Jacob (Israel) publicly recognized the two sons
born to Joseph from his Egyptian wedlock, and pro-
claimed them as his own children, thus conferring on
them the right to be known as Israelites: "And now thy
sons, Ephraim and Manasseh, *which were born unto
thee in the land of Egypt* before I came unto thee into
Egypt, *are mine as Reuben and Simeon,* they shall be
mine." (Genesis 48:05) They thus became a part
of the Israelitish race, and founders of two of the
twelve tribes of Israel. To further pursue this phase
of the subject, let us take into consideration the word-
ing of Jacob's dying blessing, in which he used the remarkable language to Joseph whom he called "the
shepherd and the stone of Israel," and added that
he was "a fruitful bow *whose branches run over the
wall.*"

We find that the oldest Hebrew authority, the Book of Job, discovers Job dwelling in Uz, the neighboring boundry of Canaan and the Jews themselves claim Job to have been King and High Priest of Idumaea. This would have placed him and his people in the Northeast corner of the Desert of Arabia, within social rub and touch with the Chaldeans (Hamitic). Aristeus, Philo and Polyhistor declare that Job married an Arabian whom Xenophon and Herodotus both declare to have been an Ethiopian. As we find Job in no military excursions, and must recognize his reign as a peaceful one; and he was in fellowship with the Shuhites, the Temanites and the Naamathites, three of whom the Bible calls "Job's friends"; and as we are informed by history that the people of the land of Idumaea (Edom) openly fought with the Israelites, we are brought up to the conclusion that they had become estranged from the Hebrew policy and were in such friendly relationship with their Chaldean and other Hamitic neighbors as intermarriage alone would suggest.

The Jews in Egypt caught their plans and intermingled and intermarried at will with the Egyptians. It is known that the Jews—even in their earliest military career—married among the Canaanites; they were visited, so we learn from Holy Writ, with pestilence upon pestilence therefor. It is universally allowed that the Phoenicians were Canaanites by descent. The Carthaginians, Numidians, Mauritanians, Gaetulians, Melanogaetulians and Ethiopians were Africans, and *Phoenician merchants took wives among them and led their families into intermarriage.* Philistus, of Syracuse, a writer of good authority who lived over 350 years before Christ, relates the *first traces of Carthage were owing to Zorus and Charchedon, two Tyrians or Phoenicians,* thirty years before the destruction of Troy, according to Eusebius. Here we seem to have a direct introduction of Jewish blood into Africa.

Continuing the subject of intermarriage from the study of the principal individuals of Jewish history, David's example has special significance here. Let us bear in mind that David was the direct descendant of Rahab the harlot, who, having saved the spies, was afterwards taken safely into the Israelites' faith and married *to Salmon the son of Naashon,* and the *great-grandfather of David. This same Rahab was the mother of Boaz,* and was a Canaanite, as we know. The Author might add, however, that the Hebrew word "Zonah" means an innkeeper rather than a harlot, and it is probable Rahab was merely the keeper of a public hotel rather than a house of ill repute.

In this connection a stronger instance of reckless disregard for the Hebrew law against intermarriage may be mentioned. Ruth, notwithstanding she was a Moabitess, was taken to wife by Boaz, although his father *was a priest of Judah,* and the law expressly forbade marriage to a Moabitess even to the tenth generation. The Carthaginians were Negroes; Eusebius and Procopius are positive that the Canaanites who

fled from Joshua retired thither, and St. Austin would
have it believed that the Carthaginians were descended
from the Canaanites. David was on friendly terms
with the Kings of Gath (Hamitic), visited among
them and while he was in Ziklag he was joined by a
great force of the tribes of Benjamin and Judah who
crossed over the Jordan and dwelt with David in Ziklag for several years. History says: "multitudes of
valiant men, commanders out of the tribes of Benjamin
and Judah, and Saul's kindred besides some of the
tribe of Manasseh," etc. Bear in mind that the Amalekites came up at this time and carried away all their
women, children, cattle and all the plunder of the
place, for repeopling their families (just previously
spoiled by David) and it is not likely they would have
feasted for two days and nights as they did without
having had intercourse with the women of the Israelites whom they had captured for this purpose, as is
very evident. It was some time before David overtook
them, and as their custom was to kill all the women and
children outright, which they did not do in this instance, they were intent on retaining them for the
reestablishment of their own nation. Although these
were afterward rescued, it was not until after violence
had been done their women folk by the Amalekites. The
Amalekites were descendants from Esau by his concubine Timna, and therefore Hamitic, for (Genesis
36) "Esau took his wife of the daughters of Canaan,"
and his concubine likewise. As conquerors had the
privilege of intercourse with their female captives, we

must conclude that this military excursion produced a blended race; the Arabian historians go even further and reckon Amalek a descendant of Ham. It might be well to remember, just here, that the modern Arabians, especially those who are Mohametans, still practice circumcision as it was done in their most ancient days.

Josephus seems to believe David's marriage to Maacah, the daughter of Tolmai, King of Geshur, was a marriage outside the Semitic fold. David had two children at least by her; history is positive that Geshur was a portion of Syria in which both the Hamitic and Semitic races had blended, for one eminent authority says: "It was the most ancient settlement. This is indisputably the case. But the posterity of Shem (by Aram) did not possess this country wholly to themselves; their relations of Canaan's line being straitened for want of room in the places where they settled at first, encroached upon them by degrees and seized a portion of their lot and kept the same until one common destruction and captivation involved them both. * * * We find a very noted portion of Syria denominated from one of the eleven sons of Canaan *who may have even settled here in person.* * * * We can only deliver it as our opinion that the Canaanite families did, most if not all of them, fix their abode in Syria. But whether the country was more or less divided among the Aramites and Canaanites we forbear to inquire into since we have little or no authority to build upon.

"The ancient Syrians, then, were partly descended

from Ham and partly from Shem and both of nearly
equal standing in this country." To confirm this the
Arabs have a tradition that Canaanites (Hamitic)
were originally in Syria. Justin reckons Abraham to
have been at one time a king in Assyria. Cleric and
Bishop Patrick (in their notes on Samuel) affirm the
Geshurites *in the day of David to have been Canaanites.* Isaiah (11:11) speaks of the "remnant of his
people which shall be left from Assyria, and from
Egypt, and from Pathros, and from Cush, and from
Elam, and from Shinar, and from Hamath, and from
the islands of the sea." So we have ample evidence,
it would seem, that they were of Negro blood. That
David should have intermarried with them suggests
its own conclusion. David had in all, sixteen wives.

It would seem that Solomon, the wisest of all the
ancients or moderns, and the direct son and successor
of David, would have been more careful of the regal
line than to have broken into the irrefragable customs
of monarchy to marry out of their prescribed and
legally ordered circles. Whatever the religious scru-
ples of monarchy, or whatever may be monarchy's
peculiar weaknesses of dissipation, the ceremonies of
wedlock have ever been their chief concern when it
may affect the regal line, and they have hesitated to
marry out of their circle. Yet Solomon married the
daughter of Pharaoh, King of Egypt, and this gives
us another instance which supplies evidence of the relationship existing between the Egyptians (Hamitic)
and the Jews even in so late a day as that of Solomon.

Pharaoh not only gave Solomon his daughter in marriage but also conducted a number of military excursions against the Philistines in Solomon's behalf, and gave other instances to show that there was a close affinity between them. It was at this period of history that the Amorites, Hittites, Perizzites, Hivites and Jebushites were reduced to the grievous state of bondage and slavery whence it is gathered that they were brought so low as to be unable to answer the demands of tribute, wherefore, being admitted into a covenant with King Solomon, they were employed in the heavy labor of carrying on his vast and sumptuous work; and it is very apparently certain that they were upon their first reduction made PROSELYTES TO THE JEWISH RELIGION, and thus they are thought to have been blended with the Jews, for the text is very definite and obvious: "And all the people that were left of the Amorites, Hittites, Perizzites, Hivites, and Jebushites which were not of the children of Israel (another instance of indiscriminate blending) their children that were left after them in the land whom the children of Israel also were not able utterly to destroy, upon these did Solomon levy a tribute of bond-service," etc. Elsewhere we find mention of these as the children of the Canaanites, which indicates that this blending was directly with the offspring of Ham. In another instance we are referred to certain texts of Scripture bearing directly on this subject, and Josephus, the Jewish historian, after enumerating those who returned from Babylon, *reckons up six hundred and fifty*

*who passed for Israelites, but could not make out their
extraction.* One author, speaking of this remarkable
condition of miscellaneous blending on the part of the
Jews and Hamites, says: "Josephus also found others
of uncertain genealogy and servants that attended upon
the whole multitude to a great number, there being in
all about eight thousand enumerated by Josephus.
But this number is still too small, as these were in all
probability Canaanites, but the far greatest part of
the better sort were blended with the Jews so intricate-
ly that there was no distinguishing between the preten-
tions of each, and moreover multitudes had remained
behind in the place of their captivity." (In this he
means multitudes of those who had blended with the
Jews, as he explains elsewhere).

The Abassines are firmly persuaded that the celebrated Queen of Sheba who had an interview with
Solomon, reigned over the proper Ethiopia. They
have a history of her written at large, but interspersed
with various traditions. The substance of this history
is as follows:

Makeda, for according to them that was her name,
receiving an account from Tamerin, an Ethiopian merchant, took a journey to Jerusalem to know the truth
of this report. She was attended by a great train of
her prime nobility and carried with her a variety of
most magnificent presents. After she had been instructed at Jerusalem in the worship of the true God,
she returned home and within the space of a year
brought forth a son begotten by Solomon, who named

him David, but he was called by his mother and her
subjects Menelech or Menilehech, that is: another
self. He received his education at Solomon's court,
and was accompanied home by many doctors of the
law and Israelites of distinction and particularly Aza-
riah, the son of Zadoc the High Priest. By the assistance of these Hebrew attendants, he established
the religion professed by his father in Ethiopia where
it continued until that kingdom embraced Christianity.
The Arabs and Abassines have given the princess above
mentioned, several names, as Makeda, Belkis, Balkis
or Bulkis, Neghesta Nazeb, i. e., Queen of the South,
as we find her styled by our Saviour and the Ethiopic
version, etc. The Abassines pretend that their kings
are descended in a right line from Menelech and even
most of the noble families in that part of Ethiopia at
this day trace their respective pedigrees up to Solomon.

This, then, seems to have been the prevailing sin of
the Jews—intermarriage. As early as Ezra's time
(400 B. C.) he was forced by the appearance of so
many degenerates, mongrels, and the like among the
Jews, to set about to the execution of a drastic edict
peremptorily divorcing as many of the offenders as he
could secure both from their wives and families. Here
we find the Jews marrying Egyptians, Moabites, Samaritans, Ammonites, and those strange nationalities
which had emigrated across from Ethiopia, allured by
the inviting opportunities for acquisition and conquest
afforded by a closer contact with the Egyptian people.
This "revolution" on the part of Ezra was nothing

less than a farce, however, for the people "gave their hands" to put away such wives, but the story ends (Ezra 10:19) with an acknowledgement that some of them already had children by these strange wives and even the putting away of them could not destroy the fact of the *existence* of those already begotten mongrel descendancies; besides, it is hardly to be expected that the mere formality of giving their hands would be esteemed an inviolable oath by the Jews who had so flagrantly misused the truth and personal obligation in their past history. Even Hosea (10:04) does not hesitate to say of Israel: "They have spoken words, *swearing falsely* in making a covenant." If there be any doubt as to the futility of Ezra's efforts to stop this interwedlock abuse of the Jews, it is dispelled a little later by the marriage of Esther, a Jewess, to Ashasuerus, "King from India even to Ethiopia" as is mentioned in the preface.

NEGROES AND EGYPTIANS SIMILAR.

From Frontinus it is evident that the Carthaginians had Melanogaetulian or Nigritian troops in their service before the time of Gelon, and consequently that they had some knowledge of the Blacks more than five hundred years before the birth of Christ. There are several coins in existence given us by antiquity with a Negro's head upon them, and they are explained away in this manner. One of these coins was as late as the last century in the fine cabinet of the Earl of Pembroke, and another was in the cabinet of the Reverend Mr. Wise, a learned and revered gentleman who held the position of *custos archivorum* and fellow of Trinity College in the University of Oxford. His coin was found in Tripoli. These coins would indicate not only a close business relationship between the Negroes and the Carthaginians but as well a social intercourse as these coins were doubtless struck, historians believe, as memorials of some festival occasions in the Negroes' country in honor of their neighbors.

It is the remarkable concensus of opinion of more than fifty of the most noted historians of the English and Latin speaking world that the ancient Egyptians (among whom the Jews intermarried) were exactly in physical appearances similar to our present-day Negroes. The Author quotes from their report on this subject, after having devoted considerable time to an exhaustive investigation of the matter under the tutelage of the Duke of Marlborough during the early part of the eighteenth century: "It appears from some of the most perfect Egyptian mummies now remaining that the features of the ancient Egyptians much resembled those of the present-day Negroes, which is a proof that *the latter must have been originally nearly related to the former.* The language, or languages, therefore spoken in these regions bore a great affinity at first to the Egyptian, Arabic, and Ethiopic, and may at this time probably be impure dialects of them." The above would seem sufficiently conclusive to the

Author, who has already shown the reckless intermarriage of the Jews with the Egyptians, that in so doing
they laid the early racial foundations for the Negro-
Judean peoples whom we so readily receive among us
as merchant princes, social leaders and financiers, yet
who, if history is to be believed, are as much the
offspring of the early Negroes as the less fortunate
man of color who is compelled to bear the humbler
burdens of our day. To those who would discounte-
nance these deductions the Author would say that the
ancient Nigritia was but a part of the modern Negro-
land, as we know that in early times the Negroes
(Nigritiae) went by the general name of Ethiopians.
To what has been said, writes one historian: "We
must beg leave to add that the Negroes were known to
the Egyptians, Ammonii, and Cyreneans before the
time of Herodotus. For that author when in Egypt
learned it from some Cyreneans who had the relation
from Etearchus, King of the Ammonii." This historian adds that the conclusion is therefore that the
Negroes are descended from the Ethiopians and that
the region of Nigritia was peopled very early. Another author, Leo, suggests this also. The Author
begs leave to quote here an opinion as to the migrations
of the Negroes expressed more than a century ago
by an English historian then acting as a preceptor for
a member of the royal family: "The Ethiopians on
the banks of the River Nile or near the source, observing how the adjacent grounds were fertilized by its
inundations as they increased, might follow it west-

ward, every one striving to be the first possessor of a great quantity of such excellent soil and therefore advance forward until the Atlantic Ocean put a stop to any further progress. If this be admitted, *it will follow that the Blacks are not so different from the rest of mankind* as some are willing to suppose; that their descent from Adam is easy and natural, in opposition to what our modern infidels pretend; and that their *color* is only an accidental consideration.

"As for the word Africa, or as the Arabs pronounce it, Afrikia, which seems to have been unknown to Herodotus, Aristotle, Strabo and the other most ancient Greek authors, Dr. Hyde takes it to be the same with the Phoenician word or Punic word 'Habarca,' 'Havarca,' etc., or 'Avreka;' i. e., The Barca, or the country of Barca. This our readers will allow extremely probable especially since Barca was a most remarkable part of Africa, etc."

We must not omit observing here that the first division of the world was into two parts only, viz: Asia and Europe, or the eastern and western parts, Europe comprehending both the continent now going under that name and Africa, which division still prevails among many of the Orientals. This may not only be inferred from a variety of authors, but likewise from the words "Europe" and "Asia" themselves, the former importing "occidental" or "western," and the latter "half." When that vast region now called Africa was first considered as a distinct part of the world, cannot be determined, nor whether Europe and Africa were ever joined together by an isthmus uniting Spain and Mauritania, as the Author is led to believe and as some authors suggest, claiming this isthmus was later destroyed either by design of man or the visitation of an earthquake.

DID THE NEGROES KNOW OF AMERICA?

Diodorus Siculus tells us that the Phoenicians in early times sailed beyond Hercules's Pillars along the African coast, and there meeting with storms and tempests, were carried to the remotest parts of the Ocean, and after many days came to a vast island at a great distance from Lybia, and lying very far west. The Phoenicians informed the Carthaginians of this place; the Carthaginians prohibited other nations from settling in it, they reserving it for themselves as a place of retirement if they should ever be driven from their native soil. Aelian brings Silenus expressly asserting to Midas that there was a vast continent beyond Europe, Asia and Africa which ought to be considered as islands surrounded by the ocean. These and other passages that might be extracted from the ancients induced the learned Perizonius to conclude "that the inhabitants of the old world had some faint knowledge of America *derived to them either from the Egyptian and Carthaginian traditions,* or from the figure of the earth which was not unknown to them." Can we conclude from this that the Egyptians sent of their

people so early into the American continent and that
our aboriginal inhabitants removed from the environments of invention, civilization and culture to which
they had been accustomed in Egypt; and brought into
the wild. freedom of America's vast woods lapsed into
that fierce barbarity for which the original Indian is
known to history? So eminent an authority as Mr.
Whiston declared the American Indians to have been
of Jewish descent, and asserts that they were here as
early as the days of Moses. Another authority found
among them a knowledge of the flood corresponding
to the Mosaic description, which would have favorable
bearing on the general belief that the Aborigines were
descended from the Jewish race, although drifted back
into their Nimrodian barbarity.

The Queen of Sheba, Menilehec, is known to have
borne children to Solomon, one of whom ascending on
the throne of Sheba, introduced Solomon's religion.
Josephus, Origen, St. Austin, Hugo Grotius, and other
equally learned historians have placed this celebrated
princess in Ethiopia. The Kingdom of Abassia certainly seems, according to our Saviour's description,
to answer better the queen of Sheba's country as being more to the South of, and more remote from,
Judea than Arabia where some writers fix it. A distinguished writer says: "It appears from Scripture
that some persons of distinction among the proper
Ethiopians were of the same religion with the Jews,
or nearly so, in the apostolic age, since Queen Can-

dace's treasurer, baptized by Philip, went with an offering to Jerusalem to worship God there and was not unacquainted with the writers of the Old Testament, which cannot, we apprehend, be said with so much propriety of the Arabians. This seems to us a sort of proof that the *Mosaic law was held to be of divine institution* in Meroe and the other parts of Ethiopia, dependent on it even a considerable time before the birth of our Saviour, *if not as early as the age of Solomon;* and consequently adds some weight to the arguments of those writers who have asserted that the Queen of Sheba came out of Ethiopia."

Father Calumet and others suppose the eunuch baptized by Philip to have been one of the proselytes which the Jews call a proselyte of the gate, but it must be owned that this notion seems not a little improbable since those were only confined to an observance of the seven fundamental laws of natural religion enjoined by Noah to his posterity immediately after the flood, according to the opinion of the Jews whereas we find this man pursuing, and therefore not unacquainted with, the writings of the Old Testament peculiar to the natural Jews. Besides, that a treasurer or prime minister of the Queen of Ethiopia should take so long a journey as that from Meroe to Jerusalem purely to worship God and offer an oblation to Him there seems very strange if he were such a mongrel-convert as the proselytes of the gate were, who, for the most part, if not always, resided in Judea. It is therefore much more probable, especially as scarce any instance

can be produced of so eminent a personage's being ever
found among the residing proselytes above mentioned,
who were, generally speaking, people of no figure,
much less of one who exposed himself to the veriest
dangers of so long a journey merely to worship God
at Jerusalem, that this Ethiopian had been trained up
in a religion not very different from that of the Jews.
Indeed, as he was a person of such power and authority at the Ethiopian court it can by no means be
deemed unlikely that the established religion of Meroe
at that time pretty nearly resembled the Jewish.

As the Ethiopians agreed with the Egyptians in
most of their laws, their splendid funerals, deification
of their princes, the several colleges of priests, circumcision, and in short most of their sacred and civil institutions, it is highly probable that the same arts, sci-
ences and learning, as well as religion, prevailed among
both nations. According to Diodorus Siculus, the laws
of Ethiopia agreed in substance with those of Egypt.
This, continues the same author, the Ethiopians accounted for by asserting that Egypt was first peopled
by colonies drawn out of their country. Indeed, Diodorus Siculus asserts that not only the same kind of
statues but likewise the hieroglyphic figures and characters were used in Egypt and Ethiopia; since it is
generally allowed that those were the repositories of
the Egyptian wisdom and literature, and that there
was a great affinity between the Egyptians and Ethiopians in most points of importance seems to have been
the general sentiment of the Romans as well as the

Greeks, as implied by Festus when he calls them Aegyptini. Homer also celebrates their wisdom and religion when he makes Jupiter and the rest of the gods attend their entertainments. That they even were instructed in several branches of literature by Moses himself who "was learned in all the wisdom of the Egyptians" may be collected from Artopanus in Eusebius, Josephus, and others. Diodorus relates that the Egyptians learned the custom of deifying their kings from the Ethiopians, and, according to him, the Egyptians derive statuary and even their letters themselves, from the same source. This author also observes that the Egyptian and Ethiopian priests as well as kings wore caps wreathed around with serpents called asps; by which was intimated that every person guilty of treason would as surely suffer death as if he had been bitten by that poisonous animal.

There will be those who claim that these people were *not* of the Negro type as we are accustomed to-day to recognize the application of the term. According to various authors the proper ancient Ethiopians were, for the most part, perfectly black as we find their posterity at this day, though some particular cantons were white, called by Pliny "white Ethiopians." It is probable they were pleased with their natural color and preferred it to those of other nations. Some writers affirm the children of the present Abassines are terrified at the sight of an European as much as the English people are at that of a Negro, and that they paint the devil white in order to ridicule all complexions of, or bordering on, that color. Others relate that in some provinces of Abassia the people are an olive color; that in general they are born white with a black spot upon their navel, which in a short time after their birth spreads over their whole body; and that being transported into Europe they become white at the second or third generation. Gregory, the Abassine, informed Ludolphus that his countrymen came into the world of a reddish hue but in a short time turned black. Their women are strong and lusty, and bring forth with little pain as usually happens in warmer climates. When they are in labor they kneel down upon their knees, as the Hebrew women do, and are delivered without the help of a mid-wife. "Many, if not all of these particulars undoubtedly held equally true of the ancient Ethiopians," wrote Diodorus Siculus, in his comments upon these subjects.

Herodotus, himself, in describing these people informs us that Xerxes had not only eastern and western or Asiatic and African Ethiopians in his army but likewise Libyans. The eastern or Asiatic Ethiopians, he tells us, anointed one part of their bodies with a species of gypsum or plaster and another with minium or red lead immediately before they came into a general action. The Libyans, from his account of them, seem to have been Negroes, who, by Diodorus Siculus, are called Ethiopians. That author gives us the following description of them: "They are," says he, "flat-faced, exceedingly fierce and cruel in their manners, resembling beasts, extremely wicked, and have frizzled hair.

Their bodies are nasty and loathesome, their voice shrill and their disposition such as renders them incapable of being civilized. Some of them carry shields made of the raw hide of an ox and short lances in their wars; others use darts forked at the ends together with bows four cubits long, out of which they discharged their arrows by the help of their feet. When their shafts are spent, they fall on with clubs. Their women, likewise, until they arrive at a certain age, take on in the service and many of them hang a brass ring at their lips, some go always naked, sheltering themselves from the scorching rays of the sun with whatever falls in their way. Several cover their pudenda with sheep tails and others apply beasts' skins to that use. Lastly, it is not uncommon among this people to wear a garment about their loins made of human hair, their sheep in this country carrying no fleeces at all. They feed for the most part upon the tender shoots of trees, the roots of canes, the lotus and sesamus together with another species of fruit produced in marshy places. Many also live upon fowl which, being excellent archers, they kill in vast numbers. But most of them use flesh, milk and cheese for their sustenance."

As Diodorus intimates above, many of these, too, have been seated in the heart of Africa as well as on both sides of the Nile and expressly calls them Blacks, we doubt not but he had the Negroes here in view, as well as some of the proper Ethiopians; in fact, as he seems to join together the heart of Africa and both sides of the Nile, and the description he gives of the Blacks on both sides of the Nile agrees in most particulars with the present Blacks.

In another part of this book, we have given a more elaborate description of the descendants of Abraham through Ishmael. It might be well to also introduce the information that Ishmael married the daughter of Modad, a reigning prince of the Arabian line, of Jurham, and she bore him twelve sons who became rulers of Arabia. These, according to Washington Irving, drove out of Arabia the primitive stock of Joctan. (See Irving's "Life of Mahomet") This refutes the statement of those who deny that Hamitic people inhabited and permanently settled Arabia. This, we might observe, too, was in direct fulfiillment of the prophecy of Genesis 17:18, 20.

The New York "Sun" some years ago, published a scholarly disclosure of an attempt to trace the origin of the musical air to "My Country, 'Tis of Thee," our National hymn, and claimed: "it, or something like it was sung by the Jews and borrowed by them from the Egyptians in their earliest times." Thus it would seem that the very airs of our nation bear testimony to the pro-Egyptian tendency of the Jews.

WILL THE JEWS CONTROL AMERICA?

The reason the Jew has prospered and the Negro has retrograded in the United States is altogether a climatic one. They have (the Jews), by intermarriage with other nations produced a semi-blond condition which particularly fits them for the United States. The Negro, on the other hand, must eventually die out, for the African Black cannot long withstand the "sunshine hunger" of the United States as the anthropologists describe it. Dr. R. A. Katz states that the tissues demand some light stimulant, and speaks of a "light hunger" as a result of darkness. The Black Negro seems to suffer from this hunger in the United States, and enjoys nothing better than to sleep in the direct rays of the sun for it gives a feeling of extreme comfort.

To this feeling, strange to say, the anthropologists have credited the Jews' spirit of restlessness—especially those of the first generation from the Orient in this country. That feeling, too, is the cause of their gathering into the cities which are warmer; more heat being thrown out by the accumulation of buildings both in Summer and in Winter, as we know. The Jew—even of to-day—cannot withstand the cold so well as the Caucasian of the Scotch, Irish and other Aryan types. They must dress more heavily in winter. This we all know. Dr. Woodruff discusses this topic in his work, "Effects of Tropical Heat on White Men," page 171, and says: "Cities with a few exceptions show a decidedly greater brunetteness than surrounding rural districts."

If it be claimed by opponents to the Author's contention, that our earliest ancestors were all Black men (an opinion based entirely on the tropical locality of the resting place of Noah's Ark), the Author may be permitted to quote Dr. Woodruff as declaring that while the first men were doubtless brunette and that this brunetteness is still occasionally retained as a vestigial character even until some months after birth (who of us have not seen babies, born with black hair which subsequently became flaxen?), he says: "We can safely deny that the first men were Black," and he adduces reasons in accord with the accepted theories of anthropologists.

The Jews have not remained long stationary in one climate, especially in the tropical ones—and therefore have not become subservient (if this word may be employed in this sense) to those physical modifications wrought upon the Negroes.

DEGENERACY OF THE TROPICS.

The deterioration in ancient times must have been the same as in modern times, and we have an excellent example of this in Liberia. In a report made to the State Department, Ernest Lyon, United States Minister to Liberia, dwells on the physical and moral degeneracy of foreigners in that country, and the methods of some of the missionaries. Mr. Lyon says : "It is astonishing how quickly the foreigner degenerates in Africa. He is, himself, conscious of the degeneracy, but is apparently powerless to overcome the downward tendency. Climatic conditions influence the mental and moral as well as the physical and social environments. Men and women who come to teach and to lift up, have been found among the victims, not merely of heathenism, but of wanton immorality. Many of the missionaries have adopted the barter system in their work among the natives. This places the missionary on the same level with the trader," etc.

The important point, so far as climatic zones are concerned, is the fact that nearly all the territory of the United States lies within the Semitic belt. The Semitic flow has been completely reversed and is now westward across the Atlantic, and it began when we declared that all men were equal and we opened the flood-gates to our present sorrow. It does not require inspiration to prophesy that this type will outlive the blond Aryans eventually, that the aristocratic democracy now being evolved will fall into its tender mercies, as in Greece, Rome, and India—providing, of course, the blond immigration is not re-established.

No great disasters need be anticipated, for the course of history only shows that American destinies and civilization will be upheld from the Northwestern corner of Europe, just as that corner is upholding the civilization of the rest of the Semitic belt. Americans will be just as contented and happy as now, and we need not worry about posterity—not in the least. Egyptians appear to be happier than they ever were when they were independent of Northern control.

WAS CHRIST A JEW?

The contemplation of this inquiry we must assume with the greatest reverence and regard. We are too prone to familiarize with God and His providential Heir. There is too readily a flippancy in the assumption of acquaintance with God and Christ. The name should inspire awful reverence, and should be treated with respectful silence often when we assume to use it lightly. No sect handles the Omnipotent's titles so recklessly as do the Christians. Republicans mostly in our tastes, we are irreverent in our regards. That men should give utterance to the name of the Most High except with awe and solicitude is astounding; that men should connect that same great Being with their violence of passion and of rage, and swear in the name of God Almighty is dreadful to contemplate. We know nothing of God, save the pittance His Omniscience has vouchsafed us in our weak and puny lives. We are but atoms in His sight, and we are puffed up that He should have created us, and think ourselves stupendous that He should have sent His Only Begotten Son to die to redeem us. The Author confesses to a feeling of indescribable and inexpressible reverential gratitude at the mention of God's name, and a shrinking introspection of his own littleness in the knowledge of Almighty Christ. That man should take the name of God in vain, sends the chill of death into the heart and stupefies the contemplative brain. God! Maker and Master of all that lives and moves; Creator of

Suns and Moons, Master of Destinies and King of
Kings! He at whose nod the mightiest potentate
shrivels into his shroud and returns to elemental dust;
with pomp and pageantry of kings but the vanity of
God's Imperial Court. We gather the wisdom of the
heavens and the earth, go down into the unfathomed
depths of the seas and amass the intelligence of wasted
ages—only to behold that it is foolishness with God.
We stand out under the bright canopy of the beauteous
night, and reckon the myriad stars that reflect the
magnitude and magnificence of His gigantic creative
power, and say with the Psalmist: "What is man that
Thou art mindful of him?" We study the systems of
creative genius, enter into the depth of science, and are
impotent to recreate the smallest living germ that grov-
els at our feet. We breathe the inspiring air, but all
our science cannot behold it nor stop it in its course
from place to place. We shudder at the approaching
day of death, yet all of our wisdom and our ingenuity
cannot stay the moments of time, nor govern the movements of a single element of God. Who lit the teeming
stars and kindled the flames of passion and of love?
Who set the mighty day-sun in his course, and regu-
lates the movements of the nightly moon? Who set
the bounds of sea and land, and with His whisper
stilled the raging storm? Who heaped the monu-
mental mountains in their place and filled their base
with the riches of silver and of gold? Who laid the
measures of the earth or stretched the line upon it?
"Whereupon are the foundations thereof fastened, or

who hath laid the corner-stone thereof, when the morning stars sang together, and all the sons of God shouted for joy?" "Or who shut up the sea with doors, when it brake forth as if it had issued out of the womb? When I made the cloud the garment thereof, and thick darkness a swaddling band for it, and brake up for it my decreed place, and set bars and doors, and said hitherto shalt thou come but no further; and here shall thy proud waves be stayed. Hast thou commanded the morning since thy days; and caused the dayspring to know its place? That it might take hold of the ends of the earth, that the wicked might be shaken out of it. Hast thou entered into the springs of the sea? Or hast thou walked in the search of the depth? Have the gates of death been opened unto thee? Or hast thou seen the doors of the shadow of death? Where is the way where light dwelleth, and as for darkness, where is the place thereof? Hast thou entered into the treasures of the snow? Or hast thou seen the treasures of the hail? By what way is the light parted, which scattereth the east wind upon the earth? Who hath divided a watercourse for the overflowing of waters, or a way for the lightning of thunder, to cause it to rain on the earth where no man is; on the wilderness wherein there is no man; to satisfy the desolate and waste ground, and to cause the bud of the tender herb to spring forth? Hath the rain a father, or who hath begotten the drops of dew? Out of whose womb came the ice? and the hoary frost of heaven, who hath gendered it? Canst thou lift up thy voice to the clouds, that abundance of water may cover thee? Canst thou send lightnings that they may go and say unto thee, Here we are? Who hath put wisdom in the inward parts? Or who hath given understanding to the heart? Who can number the clouds in wisdom, or who can stay the bottles of heaven? Hast thou given the horse strength? Doth the hawk fly by thy wisdom and stretch her wings toward the South? Doth the eagle mount up at thy command, and make her nest on high? Hast thou an arm like God? Or canst thou thunder with a voice like Him? Hell is naked before Him and destruction hath no covering. He stretcheth out the north over an empty place, and hangeth the earth upon nothing. He bindeth up the waters in His thick clouds; and the cloud is not rent under them. He holdeth back the face of His throne, and spreadeth His cloud upon it. He hath compassed the waters with bounds until the day and night come to an end. The pillars of heaven tremble and are astonished at His reproof. He divideth the sea with His power, and by His understanding He smiteth through the proud. By His spirit He hath garnished the heavens; His hand hath formed the crooked serpent. Lo, these are parts of His ways; but how little a portion is heard of Him? But the thunder of His power, who can understand? He rebuketh the sea and maketh it dry, and drieth up all the rivers. The mountains quake at Him, and the hills melt and the earth is burned at His presence, yea, the world and all that dwell therein."

To confer upon the Messiah any relationship to physical infirmities is sacrilegious and unwise. It is violence to Biblical revealed truth and unfair to the proper realization of His wondrous deed. That Jesus Christ was and is co-existent with God is a truth confirmed by the revealed word of God, the prophecies, and His salutary teachings to the world. Christ was no more a part of Jewry than was the breath of life a part of Judas Iscariot. In John (17:05) Christ prayed to Jehovah: "O, Father, glorify thou me *with the glory* which I had with Thee *before the world was.*" To accept the divinity of the Christhead is to rationally dismiss the belief of any physical or racial relationship whatever. In John (IX:35-37) Jesus Himself propounded the question, "Dost thou believe on the Son of God?—It is He that talketh with thee." And in John (IV:09) we read: "God *sent* His only begotten Son into the world," and again, in John (I:1) *"In the beginning* was the Word, and the Word was with God, and the Word was God. The same was in the beginning with God." If we wish, still, to pursue the Biblical texts, we read again (Col. II:09) "In Him dwelleth *all* the fulness of the Godhead *bodily.*" Revelations (1:08) "I am Alpha and Omega, the beginning and the ending, saith the Lord."

Christ, again, in speaking of this very matter, said: (Luke XX:41-45) "And he said unto them, How say they that Christ is David's son? And David himself saith in the book of Psalms, the Lord said unto my Lord, sit thou on my right hand, till I make thine enemies thy footstool. David therefore calleth him Lord, how is he then his son?" And, when the question of his relationship was raised (Matthew XXII:42-45) Christ forever set it at rest in this language: "What think ye of Christ? Whose son is he? They say unto him, the son of David. He saith unto them, How then doth David in spirit call him Lord, saying, The Lord said unto my Lord, sit thou on my right hand till I make thine enemies thy footstool? If David then call him Lord, how is he his son? And no man was able to answer him a word."

Again, John (X:30) "I and my Father are one." Revelations III:14, calls Christ "the beginning of the creation of God." We also find Christ credited with the creation of all things. John (I:03) says, "All things were made by Him, and without Him was not anything made," and in verse 10: "the world was made by Him." Col. I:16-17) "By Him were all things created that are in heaven and that are in earth, visible and invisible, whether they be thrones or principalities or powers, all things were created by Him and for Him; and *He is before* all things, and by Him all things consist." Again, we find in Proverbs (VIII:-23) "I was set up from everlasting, from the beginning or ever earth was," and once again in John (VIII:58) "Before Abraham was I am." The New Testament has incorrectly translated Paul (Hebrews II:16) when it makes him say of Christ: "For verily He took not on Him the nature of angels; but He took on Him the seed of Abraham." The words "Him the

nature" and the second "Him" are not in the original
Greek, and the original Greek has it: "He taketh not
hold of angels, but of the seed of Abraham he taketh
hold." Christ's birth antedated the formality of the
delivery of Mary. God said (Psalms II:07) "Thou
art my Son, *to-day* have I begotten Thee." Again,
Paul (Hebrews VII:03) says: "Without father, without mother, without descent, having neither beginning
of days nor end of life but made like unto the Son of
God," and again, "who is made not after the law of
carnal commandment." How ridiculous, then, for
those sticklers after strict adherence to physical and
natural laws which made Christ delivered in full time
maternally, and graded through the steps of youth and
manhood, to impute upon Deity the physically impossible of the creature creating the creator. If Christ
made all people and all things, as is stated above, He
was the creator of Mary, who could have had no physical influence on His own creation.

God does not subject His immutable laws—even
physical—to impossible and ridiculous violations, and
the Immaculate Conception had nothing to do with the
physical; it was God's plan of miraculous advent of
His Only Son. The verses quoted above, and taken
from God's inspired word evidence conclusively the
sacrilege we do to meditate upon Christ as the physical
offspring of one of our own weak kind. Besides, we
know that Christ appeared in physical form many
times previous to His Immaculate Conception. He
appeared in physical form to Abraham, partaking of

food, and discussing affairs face to face, as is clearly stated in Moses's history, Genesis XVII. He assumed human form and stood before Moses (Numbers XIV: 14) face to face, and in Exodus (XXXIV:05) we are told this reference was to Christ since no man ever saw God. Luke (III:23) qualifies Christ's earthly relationship by saying: "Being (as was supposed) the son of Joseph." This same supposition has given us our own mediocre opinion of the Omnipotent Christ. It was this view that made a great part of the earth rank Christ merely as one of the prophets and gave Mahometanism its birth, and Confuscianism its hold upon the Orient. The whole world believes in Jesus Christ the prophet, His existence as the earthly man of high repute is known to history. But attempts to give Him earthly relationship have tarnished His magnificent name and made it a by-word among the heathen. Christ persistently instructed His followers as to His proper relationship, and once He boldly asked the question: "Who is my mother, and who are my brethren?" and answered it Himself in the words: "For whosoever shall do the will of my Father which is in heaven, the same is my brother, and sister, and mother," thus indicating He held no physical relationship.

This subject seems to have been touched upon in the conversation between Christ and the Jews who believed on Him. See John VIII:48. The Jews said directly to Him: "Say we not well that thou art a Samaritan and hast a devil?" To this Christ replied by emphasizing the fact of His existence in times previous to Abraham. The Jews of Christ's day had no relationship with the Samaritans, and the Samaritans had employed various strategems and calumnies to hinder the Jews in rebuilding the temple at Jerusalem, and when they could not prevail, they erected a temple on Mt. Gezirim in opposition to that of the Jews at Jerusalem.

One historian declares of the Samaritans of that time: "They were not of the seed of Israel, but of the posterity of that mixed multitude whom Shalmanezer, King of Assyria, sent from Cuthah, Ava, Hamath, Sepharvaim and other provinces to inhabit those parts." The Samaritans themselves claim their origin to be from Joseph by Ephraim. Ephraim was the son of Joseph by the daughter of Potipherah, priest of On, who, we have learned elsewhere, was not Hebrew but Egyptian. We are told (Acts VIII) that the Samaritans were not converted to Christianity until the ministry of Philip, Simon Magus, and Peter and John, some time after the crucifixion of Christ.

That Christ was changed by His assuming physical appearance in order to reveal Himself tenderly to mankind is thoroughly denied in the expression in Hebrews XIII :o8, "Jesus Christ, the same yesterday, to-day, and forever." The Author is quite aware there are those who will see in this view a lessening of the fulfillment of the prophecies; yet how they can arrive at this conclusion by any consistent reasoning is mysterious to the Author. We are utterly unable to under-

stand the Immaculate Conception. It is a dispensation
of Omnipotent Providence which mankind must accept through its results, recognizing the indubitable
proofs of the fact that it *is* so.

> "Presume not God to scan;
> The proper study of mankind is man."

We know that Christ held no physical relationship
to Joseph, husband of Mary, for Matthew I:18 tells
us: "Now the birth of Jesus Christ was on this wise:
When, as his mother Mary was espoused to Joseph,
before they came together, she was found with child
of the Holy Ghost," and the twenty-fifth verse of this
same chapter tells us Joseph "knew her not till she
had brought forth her first-born son, and he called his
name Jesus." Hence, since Christ was not created by
any physical force, we must conclude Christ held no
physical relation to any race, and therefore was not
of the Jews. In God's promise to Jacob of a King
of the tribe of Judah, and to his heirs of a son of
David, no physical supremacy was intended, and a
fulfillment of *those* prophecies came with the depart-
ure of the sceptre of Judah into Herod's hands. When
Herod besought of Anthony the crown for Aristo-
bulus, who was of the kingly blood, Anthony violated
all precedent by giving it unsolicited to Herod himself,
for whom he had formed a personal admiration, and
in doing so unconsciously fulfilled the prophecy of
Jacob: "The sceptre shall not depart from Judah *
* * until Shiloh come." (Genesis 49:10). Shiloh,
the Jews always considered to mean Christ.

Christ's very physical appearances were the opposites of the physical and hereditary antecedents with which He is credited. If we may presume to enter into a discussion of the Son of God as He revealed Himself to mankind, we cannot fail to observe that He had none of the Jewish traits of physical appearance. The pictures and images of Christ are markedly blond, although we are quite certain that this type was not found in Israel. Ripley quotes Beddoe as having mentioned some doubt as to Christ's blondness, and we know that in the second century after His crucifixion, there was some dispute or difference of opinion as to the Lord's physical appearance, but as soon as the doctrine of the Trinity became definitely and surely orthodox, the opinion of Christ's appearance settled down into that of a tall blond with amber hair and beard, blue eyes, clear complexion with a delicate tinge of red, and oval face as described in the spurious letter of Lentulus to the Roman Senate. Somewhat later, He was generally believed to have been brunette, but this change of opinion corresponded with the invasion of the Teutonic tribes into the Roman Empire. They were Unitarians as a rule, who would not accept the doctrine of Christ's divinity; and He was therefore looked on as a man who must have been a brunette like the Jews in general. But as these Teutons disappeared and the Roman Catholic church was unrestrainedly in possession of the Mediterranean type of man, the Trinitarian doctrine was re-established, and Christ was again exalted into the Godhead as a blond. In some countries, as Mexico, He was always given red hair as an exaggeration of the amber color.

There are no genealogies of the family of Christ's mother, and commentators have based their reasoning that she was of the tribe of Judah on the references alluding to Christ (supposed to be her son) as the Son of David, Joseph not being His father. This is untenable and is mere assumption. Christ was recognized by those of His time, many of whom did not believe in His Godhead, as the son of David, and was so referred to by prophecy, figuratively. Otherwise, if we omit the direct lineage through the supposititious relationship to Joseph, we have no way of connecting Christ with David at all, and the prophecies concerning Him fail, as no genealogy of Mary can be ascertained. The ancients based (as indeed do the modern critics) their opinion, for it is merely an opinion, that Mary was of the tribe of Judah, upon an old Mosaic law which prevented heiresses from marriage outside their tribes. This law was the outcome of complaints lodged with Moses by the tribe of Menasseh, and we are certain it was formed for the purpose of retaining the tribal wealth within each tribe. It could hardly have embraced Mary, since she was reckoned so poor as to hardly have been numbered among the heiresses, besides the other arguments of the commentators who adhere to the belief that Mary was of the tribe of Judah and that her zeal in the belief of the promised Messiah being given through their tribe kept the sons and the daughters of Judah from marrying outside

their own tribe, seem to be at variance with consist-
ency; and this gives too slender a base on which to
found a final decision respecting so great a subject.
So we have absolutely no historic evidence that Christ
was a Jew, in direct blood connection or relationship.
If we may accept the traditions generally accepted concerning Mary's personal appearances, she could hardly
have been Jewess considering the types then prevailing and the section of country whence she came.   It
is well to recognize, too, that this traditional description is given credence by Dr. Cunningham Geikie, and
indeed is accepted by the Roman Catholic church which
paints all its portraits of the Virgin Mary after this
fashion.

Christ bore no physical relation to man in our common manner of considering this subject of kinship, as
is further shown by the fact that Joseph never had intercourse with Mary, either before or after Christ's
birth. It is chronicled of Joseph that he knew his wife
not until the time of the birth of Jesus, which is a
Hebrewism we must not overlook.   It is certain that
the particle "till" especially according to the genius
of the Hebrew tongue, does not always imply the du-
ration of a thing to such a time, but often carries a
continuation unto the end; otherwise Christ would
have His session at the right hand of God no longer
than till His enemies were made His footstool (Psalms
CX:01).   Timothy would have been obliged, according to St. Paul's exhortation to have vacated to the
Scriptures and other episcopal duties, no longer than

till the coming of the apostle to him (1st. Timothy,
IV :13) ; and Jacob would have been no longer entitled
to the divine protection than till God had performed
the promise of bringing him safe into his own home
again, (Genesis XXVIII :15). There are many similar instances which the reader may see if interested in
the pursuit of this phase of the study, in the famous
concordance of indeclinables printed by Froben. The
references to Christ's brethren (especially in Matthew
XII :47), do not indicate the physical but rather
spiritual brethren of Christ; or if we disallow this
view, we know that in this instance the reference was
made to James and Joseph, who were not the children
of Mary the mother of Christ, but of Mary of Cleophas. John (XIV :25) tells us that Mary of Cleophas,
the sister of the mother of Jesus, was the Mary at the
crucifixion, and the twenty-seventh chapter of Matthew and the fifteenth chapter of Mark show this Mary
to have been the mother of James and Joseph. The
custom of the Hebrews was to call cousins brothers,
and this appellation was often extended to other close
kinspeople. Abraham, in Genesis XIII :08, calls Lot
"Brother," and there are many similar instances. It
is believed that Joseph retained through his entire life
an absolute continence with Mary, and this is better
argued by the fact of Joseph's advanced years, as he
was an old man. It is the commonly received opinion,
founded on an ancient tradition, that Joseph died soon
after the feast of the passover, to which he and Mary
and Christ had gone during Christ's tender youth, and

where He remained behind His parents until they sent and brought Him to them, after three days of sorrowful search. This opinion is further confirmed, too, by the fact of the Jews calling Christ sometimes the carpenter, and sometimes the carpenter's son, indicating that He must have been called on to remain at home and labor at His adopted trade for the support of Himself and His mother, Mary. But we must recognize some diviner plan than humanity alone in Christ's physical revelation to us, and the fact that His mother never gave birth to other offspring. The whole plan of the Socinian and Unitarian theory—like others that have debased our conception of the Holy Christ, owes its creation to this opinion of Christ as a physical man.

Geikie says: "It is impossible to trust to the descriptions of Mary's person, but it is interesting to know how remote generations imagine her. She was in all things serious and earnest, says one old tradition, spoke little and only what was to the purpose; she was very gentle and showed respect and honor to all. She was of middle height, though some say she was rather above it. She spoke to all with a prudent frankness, soberly, without confusion, and always pleasantly. She had a fair complexion, blonde hair, and bright hazel eyes. Her eyebrows were arched and dark, and her nose well proportioned, her lips ruddy and full of kindness when she spoke. Her face was long rather than round, and her hands and fingers were finely shaped. She had no pride but was simple and wholly free from deceit. Without effeminacy, she was far from forwardness. In her clothes which she herself made, she was content with the natural colors."

In concluding this subject, the Author feels it not amiss to introduce some comments as to the erroneous impression that Christ was called a Nazarite, He having been born in the city of David, as we know. We can find no reference in any version (unless it be the Chaldee and the Syriac, perhaps) but in the original Hebrew we find Him called "Notzer." This, however, was not on account of His having received that appellation from any particular city, but by reason of His high character, office, and descent. In Exodus (XXXIV :05) where the Lord is said to descend in the cloud, and to proclaim the attributes of the Lord, it is observable that the first letter of the word "Notzer" (keeping) is one of those which the Jews call *majus cula,* or large letters, such as occur only about thirty times in the whole Old Testament. These are, according to them, never used by the sacred writers but to imply some great mystery to be contained in the word. This name "Notzer," is given to the divine person appearing there which could not be that of God the Father Whom no man has seen at any time, but of the Son in that human appearance which we know Him to have assumed, both before and under the Mosaic dispensation. Certainly none could have a better claim to the title "Notzer chessed" (preserving mercy) than He who came to obtain it at no less a price than His own inestimable life. In Isaiah (XI :01) the same Messiah is called a "Netzer," or "brand out of the old stem." Here it signifies the spontaneous shoot which springs from the branch.

The Jews had the false idea of Christ that He was born at Nazareth, and that, therefore, He was a Galilean. The Jews also felt that as no prophet had ever arisen out of Galilee, they could refute Jesus' divine claims to the Messiahship by the proof of the fact that Christ was born in Nazareth. This is why they gave Christ the name of "Nazarene"—out of derision and ridicule. It was taken up by His followers *as originally meant by Moses* and Isaiah, and hence it became attached to Christ. The Author is of the opinion this same Christ was *not* born in a stable, but that Mary was delivered in an open field, and the child Christ brought and laid into a crib. The text in Luke plainly indicates the act of carrying the child after birth into the manger (Luke II:07). But this is immaterial to the subject of this work.

WHITE MEN IN OLDEN TIMES.

The claim has been advanced by certain Jewish apologists that the close affinity proved elsewhere in this volume as existing between the Ethiopian, Egyptian, Hebrew and other types of men, was a consequential result of the *entire* absence of white men as we now know them. This is far from the recognized truth. It will not do to claim that all men were originally black or dark because born in the tropics. This begs the question and repudiates historical discoveries to the contrary. There are hieroglyphics on the Egyptian pyramids that express "white men of the North with blue eyes," and we know that these pyramids stood at least 3000 years B. C.

In the Boston museum there is an ancient Greek amphora of the earlier art age decorated with views of artisans and mechanics which shows them to be very dark, but the customer being served in a shoemaker's shop is white.

The word "Helen" means white, the Hellenes were white men and Helles was white man's country. The Trojan war seems to be a tradition of a race war, the white men being banded together to revenge the kidnapping of one of their women by the darker race.

The old Greek amphorae have a remarkable tendency to depict women with white skins, while all the other people are shown as very dark. The Author mentions this because the Greeks descended from Japhet, and were Aryans; thus it deduces a further proof that to Shem and Ham was conveyed the burden of jointly producing the black races of the world. The Author refers the reader who desires a fuller explanation of this reference to the Hellenes to Dr. Woodruff's admirable work: "Effects of Tropical Light on White People," page 235. Homer's characters were all tall, chestnut-haired, and apparently Teutons. The modern Greek by his intermarriage has become more Jewish in his cast than the ancient Greek was. This is self-evident. The present King of Greece is a *Dane;* the modern Greeks indicate that they are of Negro blood and Jewish cast.

That some Jews are white is no argument against the theory of this work. Professor W. J. McGhee, that eminent authority, who was Director of Anthropology at the St. Louis Exposition, says: "Esthetic development tends to whiten the skin. Culture would therefore tend to produce a blond race, while vigor, on the other hand, would tend to produce a brunette race." As the Negro has always been committed to the serfdom of civilization, and the Jew has engaged in the sharp practices of mental erudition, accepting the utterance of this great anthropologist, is it any wonder the modern Negro is blacker than his white brother, the Jew?

Dr. Maurice Fishberg, himself a Jew and an ethnologist and anthropologist of wide repute, and others have proved that the ancient Jews were distinctly African in type.

Just here the Author would beg leave to call attention to the Negro characteristics to be observed in the mummies of the most distinguished Egyptians, as well as to their Semitic blending. In a study of the mummies of Seti I, and Rameses II, there is seen in the features of these most renowned of the Pharoahs such a combination of the Hebrew and Hamitic casts as is astonishing. Both are strong faces of Jewish cast; with the unintellectual, slightly animal expression of the Negro. They are in such a remarkable state of preservation that Professor Maspero, the Director-

General of the Excavations and Antiquities of Egypt, declared that if their subjects were alive to-day they could not fail to recognize their old sovereigns. And yet to those of us who have observed the features of Negro corpses, especially of those who have been subjected to the unusual methods of execution known to the South, there is a striking suggestion of the similarity between these mummies and the Negroes of to-day. Examined ethnically, the outlines of the Hebrews are plainly discernible—the early relationship co-existing between the Hebrew and Egyptian (hence Negro) is self-evident.

CONCLUSION OF THE WHOLE MATTER.

And now we have come to the end. The Author believes he has established the proofs of his contention, by reason of the following:

I. By historical evidences of the early affinity of the Jews which recognized Negro races.

II. By evidence showing that racial antipathy was so much more marked in the olden time than at the present, that had the Jew not been originally Negro, or at least so early in his history as to give basis to the modern race, the social, political and commercial relations which their more illustrious leaders as have been shown in this volume have maintained, would have been improbable, if not impossible. Abraham reared a race by Hagar, an Egyptian. Job, according to history, married an Arabian Negress. Joseph married an Egyptian, daughter of Potipherah, priest of On.   Moses married a Cushite, daughter of Jethro, and according to history, Princess Tharbis of Ethiopia.   Boaz, great-grandfather of David, married a Moabitess.   David married Maacah, daughter of Tolmai, King of Geshur whom Josephus believes to have been Negro.   Solomon wed the daughter of Pharoah, King of Egypt, and also the Queen of Sheba who was an Ethiopian.   Esther married Ahasuerus, "King unto Ethiopia."

III.   By the wholesale importation, migration and intermingling of the original Jew types with the Egyptian, Arabian, African and other Hamitic or Negro races.

IV.   By the retention, even through their various migrations of similarities of speech, customs, religion and physical characteristics, especially as shown by mummified remains and in the researches of anthropologists.

V.   By the emphasis laid on, and the importance given in Biblical (Jewish) history to, visits of state by Negro monarchs and their doings over those of other nations in equally direct contact with the Jews, as follows: The advices of Jethro to Moses, which laid plans for the entire Jewish mode of judicature; the elevation of Joseph in even an earlier day to the Prime Ministry of an African government, Egypt; the visit of the eunuch Prime Minister from Queen Candace's realm to Jerusalem to receive baptism from

Philip; the visit of an Ethiopian queen to the court of Solomon, and other similar circumstances set forth herein.

VI. By a series of comparisons, both historical and ethnical, aided by an examination of miscellaneous photographs gathered by the Author from a careful study of the American Jews and American Negroes in more than twenty-eight states, which set forth such marked similarities that the Negro characteristics of the present day Jews remain notwithstanding their years of intermarriage with Caucasian types.

The Author is quite convinced that it will be difficult for the Jews of to-day to recognize their less cultured African brother, whose skin, in his racial dependency and long years of uninterrupted repose under the degenerating climatic conditions of Africa has retained its ebon hue, and whose mind has not yielded so readily to the enlivening processes of the sharp practices of trade. As has elsewhere been shown, the gradations of ethical culture, intermarriage, migration, and intimacies with Caucasian races have elevated the Jewish people to a condition where they control vast commercial enterprises, possess some social prominence, and but for their retained brunetteness, in many respects resemble the Caucasians. Yet thousands of years of effort to throw off their nigrescence have failed to eradicate those race characteristics, and the Jew of to-day is essentially Negro in habits, physical peculiarities and tendencies. The Jews who have migrated in modern times into African and other Ne-

gro countries have quickly drifted back into the habits
and conduct of the uncivilized Negro races surrounding them.

Prior to the Civil War in the United States, many
Negroes, escaping from Virginia and North Carolina
slave-owners, found shelter in the fastnesses of the
Dismal Swamp where the natural surroundings assured them protection from detection and discovery,
by their masters. It is well known that these Negroes
soon lapsed into savagery, lived on the roots of trees
and shrubs of bushes which they found there, built
rude huts in which they dwelt, and as their numbers
were augmented and their savagery increased, selected
the mightiest among them as their rulers; and they
had well nigh got into a state of cannibalism when
Federal interference came to their relief. It was with
difficulty that they were recalled into a civilized state
of existence, preferring their newly acquired barbarian
habits, although the proffered freedom brought with it
assurances of the full rights of American citizenship
and elective franchise.

Another marked similarity peculiar to the Jews and
Negroes is their aptitude in imitation. Both are great
imitators, as were their forebears in Egypt from whom
the Jews borrowed almost all their ceremonies. In
business, the Jew to-day is quick to adopt his competi-
tors' methods, and the great Jewish printing houses,
factories, and mercantile establishments are rendezvous
for heads of departments in competitive institutions
who may be secured to introduce their specialties into

the competing plants. Like the Negroes, the Jews
have no country; like the Negroes, their whole history
shows they were never capable of self-government
without direct assistance from God; like the Negroes,
they have foisted race riots on countries wherever they
have lived, and when in temporary ascendancy have
manifested their control by austerity and criminal bru-
tality everywhere. The Jews were expelled from Rome;
they were not permitted, at one time, to come within
three miles of Jerusalem. They have stirred all Europe
with their racial antagonisms. Wherever the Jew has
long had his dwelling place as a collective body of
people, he has soon precipitated the community into a
turmoil, from the time "the Jews spoiled the Egyptians" on the night of their first Passover, until their
latest disturbances in Christian Russia.

The Author firmly believes that the overshadowing
predominance of the Negro question has alone kept
the American people at peace with the Hebrews.
When—and the day is closer to hand than we imagine
—the Negro is eliminated from the citizenship of the
United States where a legislative enactment born of
impetuosity to retaliate for the wrong of slavery, once
placed him—the American government will turn its
attention to the alien Hebrew whose fomentings have
given internal disruption to the ancient empires of the
world, and who, producing nothing, has lived always
the parasitical existence. The Jews have always been
tradesmen, clothiers, pawnbrokers, and money-lenders
with the enormous extorted gains from which they

have cornered our markets, squeezed our trade, and exacted the "pound of flesh," from the days when Joseph got individual possession of the food products of all Egypt to the present day of our wheat corners, stock extortions and billion dollar trusts. The hand of the Jew is always visible—somewhere—in matters of this kind.

The Jews, like the Negroes, are pathetically devoid of regard for the truth. They esteem it thrift to misrepresent or exaggerate in a business convenience, and that "he lies like a Jew trader" has passed into a proverb. This, like his racial characteristics, however, the Hebrew has retained from inheritance. Abraham when faced with the inquiry as to his wife's relationship, deliberately falsified himself on two occasions, and yielded his comely wife to sexual debauchery in order to save himself. Providence alone saved her on both occasions from being despoiled. Moses, the lawgiver, ruler, pioneer, historian, and prince of Hebrews, did not hesitate to lie deliberately to Pharaoh, telling him they were going on a three days' journey to sacrifice to God and pledging their return with all their kith and kin within three days more. Indeed this whole Jewish race participated in it; even took advantage of it to borrow such quantities of gold, silver and age of it to borrow such quantities of gold, silver and precious jewelry from the Egyptians (and which they never intended to return to them) that the Old Testament says: "They spoiled the Egyptians." David deceived Abimilech, the priest, in Nob, when he went there (1st Samuel XXI :02) and Hushai the counselor whom David employed to secretly advise with Absolom did not scruple to deliver false counsel although it meant the weakening of Ahithophel's service and Absolom's death. These are but a few instances selected at random from Jewish history. Falsehood (not essentially malicious but for personal gain) seems almost a unit of racial characteristic among the Jews, as indeed is the disregard for the truth among the Negroes.

Other characteristics essentially Jewish and Negro are the cunning and susceptibility to bribery; and their peculiar formations of the pigmentations of the hair, eyes, and lips. Another is the peculiarity in the formation of the Jewish finger nails as compared with those of the Negro which they exactly resemble, being unlike those of other races. This is one of the most unfailing tests of Negro similarity. A study of the Negroes in fourteen states of the South and Southwest in the United States has proved that while Negroes may intermarry until not another trace of Negro relationship is visible, so long as the Negro blood is present the tell-tale finger nail formation is sure to remain. This is equally true of the Hebrew whose finger nail formation is identical with that of the Negro.

Another characteristic common to the Jews and the Negroes, and seen in no other racial division is their disregard for ancestry. Thousands of the Jews, even of the better classes, flagrantly change their names at will, as they do their religion, to better business oppor-

tunities, and genealogical considerations among them
are unknown.   Their pitiable disregard—especially
among the men—for the finer conventionalities of social life, as well as for the regularities restricting sexual indulgencies, has become a by-word.   The Jews,
like the Negroes, whom this mania often drives to
crimes against womanhood, are equally abnormally
full-blooded; but what the unfortunate Negro may ac-
complish only by brute force and crime, the Jew who
is richer, artfully effects by the gentler process of bland-
ishment, ingenuity and gold.   Of course there are
splendid exceptions to these characteristics—most es-
timable men and cultured women among the Jews who
by their contact with humanity have acquired those
finer conventionalities so pleasing to gentler society.
Both are similarly lacking in artistic taste.   Where are
there any great Jewish galleries, libraries or ethical
institutions in their name?   In music the Jews excel—
and in this exceptional case are equally similar to the
Negroes who, also, are a musical people by nature and
so far as opportunity will permit.

THE END.

CPSIA information can be obtained
at www.ICGtesting.com
Printed in the USA
BVHW040433160720
583419BV00019B/375

9 781296 621162